Thank you for downloading

How to Brand Your Home-Based Business: Why Business Branding is Crucial for Even the Smallest Startups
(The Work from Home Series: Book 4)

Sign up at my website RainMakerPress.com for special offers, promotions, and information about new releases in this series.

How to Brand Your Home-Based Business: Why Business Branding is Crucial for Even the Smallest Startups

(The Work from Home Series: Book 4)

By

Sam Kerns

RainMaker Press

Copyright © 2016 Sam Kerns. All rights reserved.

Books by Sam Kerns

How to Work from Home and Make Money: 10 Proven Home-Based Businesses You can Start Today (Work from Home Series: Book 1)

How to Build a Writing Empire in 30 Days or Less (Work from Home Series: Book 2)

How to Start a Home-Based Food Business: Turn Your Foodie Dreams into Serious Income (Work from Home Series: Book 3)

How to Brand Your Home-Based Business: Why Business Branding is Crucial for Even the Smallest Startups (Work from Home Series: Book 4)

How to Publish a Book on Amazon: Real Advice from Someone Who's Doing it Well (Work from Home Series: Book 5)

Sign up at RainMakerPress.com to receive advanced notice of new books in the series!

Table of Contents

Chapter One: Why Branding isn't only for the Big Guys 5

Chapter Two: 10 Mistakes You Never Want to Make with Your Brand 12

Chapter Three: The Difference a Decade Makes: Why Yesterday's Branding Doesn't Work Anymore 17

Chapter Four: Technology and Branding: What You Need to Know 20

Chapter Five: Let's Start Building Your Brand—Laying the Important Foundation 28

Chapter Six: Choose Your Brand's Personality 39

Chapter Seven: How Colors Affect Your Brand's Success or Failure 53

Chapter Eight: How to Create Your Brand's Identity with Logos, Taglines and More 61

Chapter Nine: How to Create a Brand Bible—and Why You Shouldn't

Skip this Step 79

Chapter Ten: How to Grow Your Home-Based Business Using Your New Brand 84

Other Books by Sam Kerns (Free Previews!) 98

Chapter One: Why Branding Isn't Only for the Big Guys

Did you know that according to the Small Business Association, 90 percent of business startups fail? That's a huge number, and although there have been many studies that show why this happens, you can boil down most of problems to one area: a lack of branding.

And that's a shame because branding a business doesn't have to be difficult or complicated. But most home-based business owners believe that branding is only for the big guys. After all, it takes a million dollars to make a business as recognizable as Coca Cola or Starbucks, right?

Not necessarily.

You see, when a large corporation sets out to brand a business, they have to do it on a nationwide—or even worldwide—scale. That takes a lot of collaboration with various professionals, PR firms, and marketing experts which obviously costs a pretty penny. But home-based business owners typically only need to brand in their local area, which is a lot less expensive and complicated. And even if you run (or are about to start) a home-based business that sells nationwide, such as an online business, you'll be able to create a brand for your business affordably using the system I outline in this book.

But this book isn't like any other branding book you've ever read. In fact, I believe small business owners should throw out everything they've ever learned about branding because folks, the times have changed. In the past, branding a business was the easy part—it was the management of that brand that made things difficult. That's because good brands were static and any type of change made to it was cause for alarm.

Welcome to the Twenty First Century.

Today, the marketplace is constantly shifting. Business owners continually face challenges such as new, unorthodox competition, fickle customers, and ever-changing marketing and business strategies. What was once a one way conversation *to* consumers is now a two way engagement *with* them. Simply put, a static brand in today's highly innovative and shifting marketplace will fall flat in the eyes of consumers.

In fact, the things I'm going to teach you in this book would have been considered heretical to good branding practices in the past decade. But today? They work. And because things are so different now, home-based business owners can easily be on the cutting edge of good and effective branding.

But before we get into the specifics, let's talk about some basics. Many people confuse the terms "brand," "identity," and "marketing," and so before we begin our journey, it's important that you understand the differences in the terms. I'll define them below, so that whenever you see them used in this book, you'll have a complete understanding of what I'm talking about.

Please keep in mind that most of the examples of real world businesses I use in this book are not home-based. That's because I want to use teaching examples with brands that everyone knows, and most home-based businesses are local so the majority of readers wouldn't know them.

- **Identity**: This is the external communications your business puts out, such as your colors, logo, and brand story. For instance, Trader Joe's, a brand that's hugely popular with Millennials, has an identity that includes Hawaiian shirts and puns printed on its products and the signs it posts around the stores. In other words, its identity is cool and relaxed.
- **Brand.** A business brand, on the other hand, is the sum of "who" your business is, what makes it tick, what it cares about, and what unique factor it offers consumers. In a nutshell, a brand is what makes up the emotional relationship

between the business and its customers. That relationship is typically built on emotions that are instilled by the brand. Trader Joe's brand is a hip store that promotes organics. And part of its brand is price—shoppers know they can afford to eat healthy at Trader Joe's because they can buy organics at a much lower price than most other stores. To sum it up, your brand is the promise you make to your customers about what they will experience when doing business with you.

- **Marketing.** Once a business has created an identity and a brand, it uses marketing to promote itself—but the marketing should stay consistent with both of them. For example, Trader Joe's sends out monthly "Fearless Flyer" newsletters that are in perfect harmony with its identity and brand.

Now that we've defined the terms that are the foundation of this book, let's talk about why a small businesses, particularly home-based businesses, should even worry about a brand.

Building a Small Business Brand—What's in it for Me?

Before we begin talking about the benefits associated with having a killer brand, let's clear up one of the biggest misconceptions I've heard. Many home-based business owners don't believe they need a brand because they "only" operate a small business out of their home. But the truth is that every business already has a brand.

That's right—if you interact with customers by selling them products or services, **you have a brand.** In other words, customers already have an opinion about your business. They think they know what it stands for, what benefits they get when buying from you, and more. But how is that possible if you've never deliberately set out to brand yourself?

Think back to our definition of a brand. It's the emotional connection between your business and your customers, and unless you've intentionally designed and guided your brand, you will acquire one by default. For example, imagine an affordable lawn business that isn't consistent about showing up on time or has a habit of missing scheduled mows. Its brand is that of a cheap company that isn't very reliable. That's probably not what the owners had in mind when starting the business is it?

On the other hand, if the lawn company had been diligent about doing good, quality work on time and always attending to its customer's needs, its by-default brand would be quite different.

So, why should you create your own brand when you can get a good brand by simply doing good work? Because, as the owner of your home-based business, it's up to you to shape your brand and then consistently tell the world about it. It's your brand, and if you plan and execute it correctly, it will take your business to the next level. Why would you leave something so important to chance?

Now that we can do away with the school of thought that home-based businesses don't need a brand, let's talk about the benefits you'll get from creating a brand and using it to grow your business.

Eight Benefits of Creating a Killer Brand for Your Home-Based Business

Remember when I said that without a brand a home-based business won't have the best chance for success? I meant it. Building a business brand will give you more than just an identity or a cool logo. A good brand can propel a business to new heights and build a loyal customer base, which will of course increase your sales. Here are ten great benefits you'll reap from building a killer brand.

Customers Will Know What to Expect

Do you know why most businesses strive to create a brand? They want consumers to know what to expect when they do business with them, and a consistent brand helps accomplish that. For example, most Trader Joe's customers would be shocked to walk into the store and find high prices because it wouldn't be consistent with the brand they've grown to trust. But they won't because the store has made a promise to its customers with their branding, and so when they walk through the door, they find exactly what they've come to expect. Once you create your business brand, your customers will also know what to expect when doing business with you.

You'll Experience Increased Sales

When customers know what to expect from a business, they typically patronize it time and time again. Just think about the local restaurant you go to for every special occasion with your family. You likely go to the same restaurant every time you want to celebrate something because you know the food will be good and the wait staff will be attentive to your needs. That restaurant enjoys your repeat business because it lives up to the promise of good food and great service. The same will hold true for your business once you've established your brand. You'll earn repeat customers who come to rely on your promise, and that will translate into increased sales and higher profits. Which leads to our next benefit...

Customers Will Remain Loyal During Rollouts

I want you to imagine two very distinct types of businesses. The first is a home-based accounting business that has put a lot of thought into branding, and has worked to ensure that people in the marketplace not only recognize the brand, but also have come to trust it. The second accounting business has put no thought into branding the business, but instead, works hard at just trying to keep up.

Now, these two business owners have never ventured beyond basic accounting, so when tax season rolls around, each owner decides to let their customers know they are adding tax returns to their services. I can easily predict what would happen next. The business owner who decided that branding wasn't necessary would have to work very hard just to convince his regular customers that he is qualified and able to do their taxes for them. But the business owner who had worked hard to brand her business as a reliable and trustworthy accountant would likely have to expend very little effort to win the increased business.

The same is true for any type of business that rolls out a new product or offers a new service. Once your branding is in place, it will do the selling for you. Remember the saying, "Your reputation proceeds you?" Branding is your reputation, and if done correctly, it will make rolling out new product offerings much easier.

You'll Achieve Greater Recognition in the Marketplace

There are always businesses in local areas that are well-known among residents. Whether it's a house cleaning agency with a stellar reputation, an on-site pet grooming business, or a plumber, the locals all know who to call when they need those types of services. And the reason their names are so well known? Branding.

I can hear some of you saying that the reason all the residents call one particular plumber is because the company is known for doing good work. Yup—that's their brand. Or maybe they call the on-site pet groomer because they feel like their pets can be trusted with the groomer. Uh-huh. That business likely worked hard to build that reputation. (Aka brand)

As you build your brand in your local community, or in your online store, you'll become more familiar to your potential customers, which will cause them to remember your name. And when it comes time for them to purchase the product or service you sell, you'll be at the forefront of their minds.

You'll Look Like a Bigger Business

I don't want you to mistake what I'm saying here—there is nothing wrong with operating a business from your home. In fact, I am thoroughly convinced that it's the way of the future. As of now, small businesses employ most of the people in the United States, and as more business owners realize the conveniences and cost effectiveness of working from home, I believe the trend will continue.

However, many home-based business owners look for ways to make their businesses appear larger than it is in order to improve the public's perception of it. In my opinion, branding is the absolute best way to do that.

Think about it—when you see a polished business presentation, don't you automatically assume it's a large, established business? Doesn't it make you feel confident that the business will be around for years to come in case you need to contact them with an issue? Most people do, and today's savvy home-based business owners are branding in a way that makes their business look larger than it actually is.

Brand Equals Quality

Have you ever noticed that when people are given a choice between two products—one that is branded and another that is not—they almost always decide in favor of the branded product? It's true, and the reason that happens is that people automatically assume that when a product or service is properly branded, the quality is better. This is true for every type of product available, from local foods at the farmer's market to the custom upholstery shop operated out of the neighbor's garage. And let's not forget the immediate benefit tied into this: when people view a product as higher quality, they'll oftentimes be willing to pay more for it.

Branding Portrays Experience

People want to do business with companies they feel have experience with the products and services they offer. For instance, if you were going to hire a home-based freelance writer, would you be more likely to hire one with a branded website that exhibits experience and trustworthiness, or one who simply emails you a generic proposal with no branding? If you're like most people, the writer who has branding to back up their claims will likely win the job. This holds true with any type of business—the better a business' branding, the more customers perceive them to be experienced and reliable.

Branding Extends Your Reach

If you run a business that offers multiple product lines, such as a company that builds, services and repairs swimming pools, you can use your branding for each product and service you offer. For example, the pool company's brand and identity would be attached to each of the services they offer, which will cause many customers to buy more than one product from them. For example, if someone purchased a pool from the company and had a great experience, they probably wouldn't hesitate to hire that same brand to maintain and clean the pool.

Now that we've talked about why it's important for home-based businesses to have a brand—and the benefits you'll get from branding your small business—let's take a look at some of the things to avoid when designing your business brand.

Chapter Two: Ten Mistakes You Never Want to Make with Your Brand

It's pretty exciting to read about all the ways a brand can benefit your home-based business, isn't it? It can give you instant credibility with potential customers, keep your existing customers loyal to you, allow you to increase your prices, make people believe you're bigger than you are, more experienced, and it will cause them to trust you—which almost always results in higher profits.

Sounds like a win-win doesn't it?

But building a brand isn't as simple as deciding what you want your company to look like. We'll talk about a step-by-step plan later in this book that will help you build your brand the right way, but first, I'd like to talk about some common mistakes that many business owners make. Avoid these ten mistakes, and your brand will be more effective.

Mistake Number 1: Not Taking it Seriously

Building a brand is one of the most powerful things you can do for your home-based business, and it's not to be taken lightly. Instead, you should go into the process with the understanding that you're about to give your business a major boost, and the decisions you make while building your brand will affect it for years to come. In other words, this is serious business—the brand you build could make or break your business—so you should begin the process with that in mind.

And if you're building a brand for a home-based online business, keep in mind that brands are favored in Google's search results. That means if you build a brand for your business and keep it consistent across the web, you could rank higher in the search engine results because of it.

Mistake Number 2: Not Keeping it Simple

If you think about some of the most successful brands, you'll quickly realize one thing they all have in common: their logos are very simple.

Think of Nike's swoosh, the red letters of Coca Cola, and the McDonald's golden arches. They are all very simple, yet powerful because customers can easily recognize them. Your logo will be a part of your brand, and it should not only be eye-catching and simple, but also help tell the story of your brand. For instance, Nike's swoosh signifies the company's motto, Just do it." Coca Cola's red letters portray the energy you'll feel after drinking a coke, and the golden arches are clean, fast and simple—just like the experience McDonald's hopes its customers have when eating at one of its restaurants.

Too many small business owners try to include all of their products and services in their brand message, but that will only dilute the message. Instead, you should focus on your core product or service and create your brand around that. For instance, if you're a home-based catering business that specializes in wedding parties, but also do events for other types of events on occasion, you shouldn't tout both of them in your branding message. Focus on the wedding party theme, and then talk to customers about your ability to cater other types of parties as well. We'll talk about your business' unique selling proposition in a later chapter, where you'll be able to identify it.

Mistake Number 3: Creating a Brand That's Too Vague

While you don't want your logo and brand to be overly complicated, you shouldn't go to the opposite extreme and make it too vague either. A vague brand can easily get lost among local competitors or in the case of an online store, the thousands of other brands out there competing for the same customers. But too many small business owners play it safe and create a brand that is vague and uninteresting, which accomplishes nothing. After all, consumes are looking for exciting brands to try, and a business associated with a vague, unoriginal brand will quickly be left behind. Remember, creating a brand is your chance to tell the world what your business is about and what makes it different. Don't be vague in that statement—it's what will set you apart from the competition.

Mistake Number 4: Relying on Guidelines Instead of Principles

When creating a brand, you'll need to ensure that the image you've selected to represent your company is consistent throughout your marketing efforts. And in order to accomplish that, you'll need some guidelines to help you along the path. Before you get into the nitty gritty of your brand, establish some loose guidelines for your colors, tagline, logo, fonts, images, voice and spokespeople. Once you have a good idea of how all those components will play into your brand, you can go from there. (Don't worry, we'll cover all this and more in the step-by-step guide I provide later in the book.)

But a mistake that many people make today is allowing those guidelines to overtake the brand's promise or allowing them to stifle creativity as the brand progresses. Instead of yesterday's thinking that the guidelines are to be followed at all costs, today's savvy brand managers are guided by principles. In other words, sure, you need some loose guidelines to help you establish your brand, but the main thrust of what defines that brand in the marketplace should be driven by the principles the brand stands for.

Mistake Number 5: Not Staying Consistent with Your Brand

If you're the type of person who believes it's good to change things up every now and then, you'll need to get a new mindset when it comes to your brand. It's crucial that you never deviate from your brand once you design it and put it out into the world. For example, if you're selling your home-based product in a specialty expo, you may be tempted to change the colors of your brand in order to fit in better with the show's theme. Don't do it. The minute you change your brand, you lose all of the brand credibility you've worked so hard to achieve, and you may or may not be able to recover from it. Instead, always stay 100 percent consistent with your brand so customers can easily recognize and find you.

Now, I need to say something here—and I'll cover this more fully in the next chapter. Just because you should stay true to your core brand, that doesn't mean you should remain static. In fact, remaining static in today's interactive world just might be the kiss of death for your brand.

Mistake Number 6: Not Controlling Others Use of Your Brand

What happens if one of your business partner decides to run an ad highlighting your business, and instead of using your brand's color and style, they improvise and change it up a bit? Or imagine for a moment that an online blog runs an article about your business, but changes the colors of your logo. Even worse, how would you feel if your fiercest competitor created a new logo that looked very similar to yours? All of these types of brand-busting mistakes can be prevented if you take a pro-active approach to controlling the use of your brand. And in the case of brand infringement, like a competitor using a logo that's too similar to yours, you may have to resort to hiring an attorney to get them to halt the activity.

Mistake Number 7: Hastily Rebranding

Sometimes it's necessary to rebrand your business, but that becomes a mistake when you don't think it through and follow a well-orchestrated plan. We'll talk about the reasons some businesses might consider rebranding—and how to do it wisely—in a future chapter. But for now, know that it's always a mistake to haphazardly rebrand a business because the change will alienate some existing customers and cause others to lose their sense of connection with your business.

Mistake Number 8: Not Including Your Employees in the Process

A brand will only be successful if it is carried out in everything your business does. The branding on your business cards should match your advertisements, and they should be the same as your brochures and flyers. But many business owners don't include their staff in their branding efforts, and that's a mistake. Even if you work out of your home an only have an answering service to field calls when you're on appointments, you should train them in how your customers will expect to be treated on the phone. Remember your brand should encompass every single aspect of your business—and that includes your employees.

Mistake Number 9: Never Changing Things Up

While you don't want to frivolously rebrand your business when the mood strikes you, you shouldn't keep the same marketing materials or run the same television or radio ads for years. Remember, your brand should stay the same, but the way you present it to the world needs to be fluid and attention getting. If you hand out the same brochures for years or run the same radio spot, customers won't stay engaged and your brand—no matter how cool it is—because it will become boring to them.

Mistake Number 10: Don't Make Claims You Can't Back Up

Finally, many business owners, in an attempt to create a brand that "Wows" customers and causes them to knock down their doors, overpromise or make claims that they can't meet. For instance, don't claim that your business can increase someone's website traffic by 100 percent when marketing your services as a home-based internet marketing company unless it's true. If you oversell or make false promises, your brand will hurt your business. On the other hand, if you make promises you can keep, it will help build that all-important trust with customers, and at the same time, build your brand.

Well, there you have it—ten deadly brand killing mistakes. As we talk about the process of creating a brand for your business, I'll refer back to these mistakes to help ensure that you don't make any of them.

Next, let's take a look at the changes that have occurred in business branding over the past decade or so. I think you'll be surprised at what used to work, but doesn't any more, and how some little tweaks in your branding efforts will make your business look updated and relevant in today's environment.

Chapter Three: The Difference a Decade Makes: Why Yesterday's Branding Doesn't Work Anymore

The world of business branding has changed significantly over the past few years, but oftentimes, small businesses create a brand based on the old school rules and then wonder why consumers aren't relating to it. In today's consumer savvy world, businesses have to create a brand that speaks to consumers in the modern language they understand. In other words, your brand needs to be built based on today's standards if it's going to be a success.

Today, everyone has a brand. It's the premise behind LinkedIn where professionals are able to brand themselves, and even my niece spent some time branding herself online before she began applying for scholarships. And no business small or large would dare to go out into the world without one. But those businesses that use yesterday's rules for branding will be quickly left behind.

The truth is, business branding didn't get its start until the 1950's when the theory of "segmentation" was developed. This theory summarized that in every market, there are segments of people who are looking for different benefits from a product or service. That theory was further expanded upon in the 1960's when a researcher proved that market segments were divided by more than just socio-economic variables like income, education and demographics. This researcher proved that other factors, such as buying behaviors, motives, and aesthetic preferences could also be segmented.

Among all these studies and research results, the concept of brand loyalty came into being. Major corporations began to develop their brands even though there wasn't any research that backed up the theory that brand loyalty was real. Then a researcher named Cunningham showed that 90 percent of American households were loyal to their product brands. And another researcher named Martineau theorized that if two stores offered the same products at the same price, consumers would choose to shop at the one that best matched their own personality.

And so business branding was born. Here's a brief rundown of how the concept has evolved over the years.

- **1970's.** In this decade, businesses built their brands to portray their "position" in the marketplace. In other words, a brand's number one job was to tell consumers why their product was better in price or quality. Because the internet hadn't yet been invented, branding was considered a one way conversation: the marketers told us what they wanted us to know and we listened. This was often done on television, or when corporations acted as "sponsors" of popular events.

- **1980's.** The concept of relationship marketing was born, but it didn't translate to brand marketing until the next decade. At this point, brand marketing was still a one way conversation.
- **1990's.** Branding became more consumer oriented as marketers realized that consumers forged relationships with brands based on their own perceptions of the brand. Brands tried to "make friends" with their customers.
- **Early 2000's.** Relationship marketing continued to expand as marketers realized that a deep emotional connection is required in order for consumers to become loyal to a brand. In addition, the demand of corporate social responsibility (CSR) from consumers majorly impacted branding. This trend is a huge benefit for home-based business owners as I will explain in the next chapter.
- **Today.** Social media has exploded any and all past concepts of branding and how

it should be done are all but obsolete. I'll dedicate the entire next chapter to talk about how this cultural phenomenon has forever changed the world of branding.

After looking at the progression of branding, can you now understand why it's so important to relate to consumers in today's terms instead of yesterdays? Let me give you an example. If you were to create a brand that focused on just your price and nothing else, you wouldn't be "speaking" to today's consumer who demands so much more. We've discussed Trader Joe's as a brand that uses price in its message, but they don't stop there. It's also promoted as a hip place to shop with a casual, fun, and laid back atmosphere. Just image what Trader Joe's would have been if it had only focused on price.

Now that we have a bird's eye view of how branding has changed over the past few decades, let's talk about the one thing that has forever changed the way businesses brand themselves: technology.

Chapter Four: Technology and Branding: What You Need to Know

As we discussed in the last chapter, branding used to be a one way conversation until the 90's when consumers found a way to open a dialogue with the companies they did business with via email, the company website, or online forums. This allowed consumers to express opinions about what they did and didn't like about a company, and also allowed them to interact with the companies they did business with.

Then social media and unfettered innovation entered the picture and branding was changed forever.

You see, social media took branding out of the hands of businesses and put it into the hands of consumers. It went from a business telling consumers what they should like about a product to consumers telling other consumers what they do or don't like.

Now don't get me wrong. As a business owner, you still need to design a business brand and get it out into the world, but what happens after that is not entirely in your control. And that's why you have to play by the rules of the Twenty-First Century.

What are those rules? Let's take a look at some of the most important ones.

Give Consumers an Interactive Experience

If you only retain one thing from this book, it's this: in today's branding environment, you must allow customers to interact with your brand in a way that will make them remember you fondly. Gone are the days when you just tell them the benefits of doing business with you, or trying to be their "friend." Today's consumers long for a deep connection with the brands they use, and the best way to give them that is by allowing them to interact with your brand.

What does that mean? Perhaps the best example of brand interaction this decade was Coca Cola's "Share a Coke" campaign. In it, the company replaced the word "Coca Cola" on their logo and substituted it for the most commonly used names in the each country they ran the promotion in. They used 150 of the most common names, and eventually added more generic titles such as mom, dad, and sis. The results were spectacular. In Australia, where the campaign started, Coke sold 250 million named cans and bottles to just 23 million people. Since then, the company has launched the campaign in other countries—all to great success.

The campaign was born of a feeling that Coca Cola had become too stale and predictable in its branding. After all, it was the first big business to brand itself, and since then, it hasn't strayed from the red and white cursive logo. But no one expected such a huge success from the campaign. Social media went wild, and people were "sharing a coke" with patients in hospitals, soldiers who were overseas, and they even sent cokes to their friends on Facebook. Soon, celebrities and even other businesses were getting in on the action by taking photos of themselves "sharing a coke." The media got involved and all Coca Cola had to do was sit back and enjoy the free press. When asked why he thought the campaign was such a success, a spokesman from the company said, "We gave consumers an opportunity to express themselves through a bottle of Coke, and to share the experience with someone else. The fact that your name is on a Coke bottle, it can't get more personal than that!"

And he's right. Coca Cola created a brand campaign that was highly personal to consumers, allowed them to interact with the brand, and used social media to help drive it. In fact, the spokesman said that if he were to do anything differently when running the campaign, he would spend only a fraction of what he did on television and instead rely on social media to spread the word.

So, what takeaway can you get from this wildly successful campaign? It's the perfect example of a brand that determined to disrupt the status quo, interacted with consumers, and then relied heavily on social media to have consumers spread the word about it.

Can you see how differently you will have to approach business branding for your home-based business based on this example? I'm trying to get you to think outside the box, because if you simply create a nice logo and sit back and wait for customers to discover your brand, you're going to be disappointed.

I want your brand to rock. I want you to turn your industry upside down with your creativity and cause customers to not only notice you, but become instant fans of your business. And creating a unique, never-been-done-before interactive brand experience is the best way you can do that.

Which leads me to my second point about today's type of brands.

Keep Up with the Current Cultural Trends

In today's world, if brands don't stay relevant and keep up with current cultural trends, they are sure to lose some of their following. In other words, you've got to stay agile with your brand.

Now, I can hear some of you saying that this advice seems to contradict my previous advice about staying consistent with your brand, but it's not. You see, in the past all that mattered was consistency and focus, but today's world simply doesn't allow that. Disruption is the mood and consumers look for brand owners to shake things up once in a while.

BUT

That doesn't mean that you shouldn't keep your brand consistent and focused—it just means that you should know when to be adaptive and adjust your brand according to changing circumstances. Today's savvy brands are never complete, but always in the evolution stage. If at the end of this book you feel that you have a brand that you can use for years without ever adjusting it, I haven't done my job.

Let's look at the Coca Cola brand campaign we talked about earlier. The company didn't change its brand or go outside of its core principles when it ran the "Share a Coke" campaign, but instead it built upon its existing brand. It kept the same colors and although the company changed the font, it kept it similar. In other words, Coca Cola stayed relevant and shook things up while maintaining the essence of its brand.

In today's environment, you'll need to constantly stay on top of trends and reinvent your brand whenever you feel it going stale. You can do that with new marketing campaigns—like Coca Cola did—innovations to your products or services, or reconstructing your unique selling proposition (we'll get into this later).

So, how can your home-based business stay relevant in a world where consumers think you're wonderful on Monday and are bored silly with your brand by Friday? Here are some tactics:

- **Keep your eyes on the future.** Just because your company is cutting edge today, that doesn't mean consumers will think of it that way next week. The marketplace is in a constant flux and upheaval, and only those businesses that stay current and up-to-date with industry trends will be able to stay in the game. For example, did you ever think Airbnb would disrupt the hotel industry like it did? And how many taxi services saw Uber coming? The need to stay focused on the horizon is true whether your sell online apps from a webstore or custom wedding cakes from your kitchen. Stay current on the trends and happenings in your industry and reflect that in your brand and relevant marketing.

- **Rely on Customers for Intel.** One of the biggest issues for brands is that they take the approach that they are in the driver's seat and it's their job to tell customers what they want. **That's a huge mistake.** The brands that resonate with consumers constantly ask them questions about their needs, desires, and seek their honest feedback. And they listen to that feedback and take action on it. You should use every communication tool at your disposal to interact with consumers and ask them for input. That means in person in your store, on your website, and on all your social media channels.

- **Never stop innovating.** No matter what type of business you run, you should always looks for new ways to innovate. Whether that means creating a new and unexpected distribution channel for your products, repackaging products to look more up-to-date, creating a new marketing campaign to update your brand, or finding new ways to connect with customers, you should never allow your public efforts to grow stagnant.

Remember, in a world full of new competition, rapidly changing marketplaces, and consumers who expect more from brands—and know when they're not being authentic—you've got to be able to pivot on a dime.

Which of course, leads me to my next point.

Be Ready to Pivot in an Instant

We talked about the importance of being agile in your branding, but now I really want to drive the point home.

Let me sum it up this way: in the past, brands were static things and it was thought that if there were any changes in a brand, it was bad. The key thing to strive for was stability and guarding the brand at all costs so it would never be perceived as changing.

That's just not how things work with today's branding. Today, companies need to be agile and ever ready to shift when the marketplace calls for it.

But being agile with your brand is an art, and if you approach it willy-nilly, it just may backfire. Here are some key concepts you should keep in mind whenever you're thinking about adapting your brand.

- **Know who you are.** Before you can adapt your brand to a changing marketplace, you must have a thorough understanding of who you are and what you stand for. For instance, imagine that you run a home-based remodeling business and your core principle is finishing a project on time and on budget. You are faced with the possibility of adapting your brand when a new competitor sets up shop and advertises extremely short turnaround times that you know aren't possible to do with good workmanship. You would have two choices: you could pivot and try to match his time frames, or you could stay true to your brand and explain to customers that your projects take longer because you don't cut corners with quality. The second is the better choice because it would allow you to stay true to your brand while addressing the competitor's claims. Remember, your brand makes a promise to your customers and you should do everything in your power to always deliver on those promises. You should strive to stand by your core principles without ever statically standing still.

- **Give Back.** Millennials make up a huge portion of today's buying public, and they are adamant about buying from companies that act responsibly and give back to the world. In order to stay agile, you'll need to constantly look around and find ways to do that. A perfect example of this is Samsung's "Look at Me" program that helped autistic children recognize facial clues. The company loaded tablets with the app and then distributed them to children around the world. But just because you're a home-based business operating in a smaller environment, that doesn't mean consumers won't expect the same from you. Stay actively informed about what's going on in your community and constantly analyze how you can become a vital part of it by giving back in some way.
- **Lead.** Passive brands often find themselves in trouble because if you aren't proactive in defining and shaping

your brand, the world will do it for you. As a home-based business owner, it will be up to you to constantly push your brand into the community, defining it by your actions, values, and core promise. An agile brand never lets others define who they are, but instead takes control of the conversation and steers it in the direction they want.

- **Be Open.** Some business owners are so enmeshed in the way they've always done things that they can't see opportunity when it's right in front of their face. But in order to stay agile, you've got to be able to see what changes need to be made, and then approach them with an open mind so that you'll be able to meet your customer's needs. For instance, imagine that you run a home-based virtual assistant business, and you typically have a set schedule for each of the services you offer. But lately, you're getting more and more requests for rush orders. You could either politely explain to clients that you don't do rushes and adhere to your schedule, or you could pivot and begin offering the rush services customers are asking for. In order to stay on top of the competition and stay competitive, you've got to be open to change, responsive to opportunity, and willing to change direction quickly.

- **Listen.** In order to be agile and pivot on a moment's notice, you've got to keep abreast of what's happening in both your industry and in your local community. And the best way to do that? Constantly invite collaboration with your customers, networks, employees, partners, and communities. They're the ones who will tell you if your product or service needs updating or a fix, what the competition is doing that you're not, and what the community expects from you as a local business owner. Make it clear to your collaborators that you're open to discussing anything that's important to them, and then create easy access points so they can contact you. Doing this will not only increase your ability to be agile when needed, but you'll also establish a firm and trusting relationship with the community.

- **Be locatable.** Gone are the days when consumers used a yellow book to look for businesses in their area. These days, home-based businesses are likely to be found on their websites, social media channels, local business directories, mobile apps, and pop-up stores. In order to be agile and fluid in today's marketplace, your business should be found on all of these places and more. But just because you can be found in on all of these places, that doesn't mean you should approach each one with the same brand experience. For instance, a home-based catering business might use scrumptious photos of enticing meals on their website or Instagram, but offer a descriptive story of a successful catered party on another channel. It will be your job to make use of every channel, but to customize the customer experience for each one while remaining true to your brand. In other words, keep your brand the same, but be agile in how you present it, according to where you're marketing.

Do you see how the internet and social media has changed the way companies brand themselves? Gone are the days when business owners controlled their own brands. Today, it's up to the business owner to create their brand, and then run their business in a way that meets the promise of that brand.

So, are you ready to start building your own home-based business brand? I hope so, because in the next few chapters, I'm going to teach you a step-by-step process that will allow you to build an effective brand for your home-based business.

We'll talk about some specific steps you'll need to take in order to design your perfect brand.

Let's start by building the all-important foundation of your business brand: your unique selling proposition.

Chapter Five: Let's Start Building Your Brand—Laying the Important Foundation

Now that you understand the basics of branding and how you will have to think in order to create a brand that resonates with today's consumers, it's time to begin working on your home-based business brand. But before we get into the creative stuff, like choosing your colors and logo, you'll need to lay the foundation.

Just like with any building structure, your business brand needs a solid foundation so that everything you do from this point forward will be properly supported. This is the most important aspect of creating your business brand, and it will take some deep thinking and instinct on your part.

That foundation is called a Unique Selling Proposition (USP), and it's what will make your business stand out in the minds of consumers because it's what makes you unique.

What is a Unique Selling Proposition?

I'm not prone to writer's block, but I have to tell you—I sat in front of my computer for quite some time trying to figure out how to best tell you exactly what a USP is and why it's so darned important for the success of your brand. Why? Because the subject is seemingly simple, but in reality, deciding on yours is the most complex and important thing you can do for your business. And I want to make sure I explain it well enough so that you'll be able to take it and run with it.

So here goes...

A USP is the backbone of your business. It's the one thing that will set apart your business in the minds of consumers and if you get it wrong, your business is likely doomed. On the other hand, if you get it right, it will cement your chances for growing a wildly successful home-based business.

No pressure, right?

In a nutshell, a USP is what you stand for. This can mean different things to different types of businesses, but in a world where so many businesses are trying to be everything to everyone, it makes sense that when you stand for one thing in particular, people are going to sit up and take notice.

For example, let's look at Starbucks, a company that uses its USP brilliantly. Starbucks started as a local corner coffee shop in Washington and has morphed into the most recognized coffee shop in the nation. But it's *how* it got there that's worth looking at.

You see, Starbucks set out to make good, quality coffee and make it convenient for consumers. In fact, that's its USP—quality coffee that can be had conveniently. Now, the coffee shop offers other things like pastries, other drinks, and even some merchandise, but so do a lot of other coffee shops across the nation. But Starbucks decided to keep it simple and stand for one thing above all else—convenient, quality coffee.

That's a perfect picture of a company using a USP successfully. Now, let's look at an unsuccessful example.

Let's imagine the local coffee shop in your neighborhood. You can't remember its name because, frankly, it just doesn't stand out in your mind. They make good enough coffee and you've had pastries there a few times that were memorable. The shop also sells breakfast and lunch dishes, and along the back wall, it offers a long row of magazines for sale. But let's be honest, in your mind, it's a good place to get a cup of Joe and a pastry, but you're not going to tell all your friends and family about it, are you?

Have you figured out why yet? It's because the shop is trying to be all things to you—a coffee shop, pastry place, breakfast and lunch diner, and a place to buy all your magazines. But what if the shop excelled in only one of those things and made that its unique selling proposition?

For example, they could focus on creating the most comprehensive magazine shop in the city—making sure they have every type of magazine a person could want, including rare, vintage, and difficult to find ones. Its USP could be that it's a coffee shop that guarantees customers that they'll have a great cup of coffee along with access to every magazine known to mankind.

Or maybe the shop grows its own coffee and roasts it on premises. In that case, its USP could be farm to coffee cup, ensuring customers that they would get the freshest cup of coffee around.

Do you see how a USP can benefit a business? And how without one, you'll just be one of many home-based businesses trying to stand out in a crowd?

What do you want to be known for? What will your business stand for? These are the questions you'll need to answer when creating your own unique selling proposition. Just remember, whatever you decide, it will determine what you're known for and customers will remember it every time they see or think about your brand. Let's begin the process of building the USP that will take your home-based business where you want it to go. First, you'll need to have a complete understanding of each of the following areas.

Who is Your Target Audience?

The first step in identifying your USP is defining your target audience. You'll need to have a thorough understanding of who they are, why they buy (or should buy) the types of products or services that you offer, what needs they have that you can fill, and what benefits they'll receive by doing business with you. Here are specific steps you can take to identify your target audience.

- **Identify the problems your product or service solves.** The first step in this process is determining which problems you solve for customers. In some cases this is easy, like in the case of a landscaper. His business solves the problem of making an average yard beautiful. Customers rely on his hard work and expertise to get the yard they want. In other cases, it's not so cut and dried. For instance, if your own a business that sells birthday party cupcakes to moms, you solve a few problems. You do the work of baking, which frees up some of their time, you create great tasting cupcakes while they may not be able to bake, and you deliver the cupcakes to the party so they don't have to haul them around. (Don't worry if your business solves more than one problem because we'll address that in a minute.)

- **Identify the people who have those problems.** Once you have the problems listed, identify what type of person might need those services. The landscaper might list people with a new home, people who are remodeling, people who have ugly yards, and people who aren't physically capable of landscaping their own yard. The cupcake baker may list busy moms, working moms, and moms who don't like to cook.

- **Segment those people into lists.** Now that you have an overall idea of the types of customers who need your product or services, it's time to segment them into lists. Do this in order to make planning your marketing strategies easier (which we'll discuss in chapter ten). Use any type of list relevant for your business, such as socio-economic status, location, market sector (are they manufacturers, retailers, or consumers?). For instance, the landscaper could create two lists of people with new homes—one for people who live in the higher end of the city, and one for those who live in areas where the incomes are lower. He may decide to concentrate his efforts on just one of those areas.

- **Identify the lists with the most motivation.** Once you have all of your lists compiled, now it's time to decide which ones contain people with the most motivation because you're more likely to achieve sales by marketing to that list. For example, let's look at our landscaper again. He may have made a few lists, including one of people in high-end homes who have their houses up for sale. Obviously, these people would be motivated to have a perfectly landscaped yard because curb appeal is important when selling a home. He would mark that list as important because the people on it are clearly motivated. Take a look at your lists and try to determine which one contains people whose problems are more pressing, and who has the most to lose by not doing business with you.

- **Don't Forget About Your Current Customers.** While compiling data on potential customers, it's easy to forget that you likely have a gold mine of information at your fingertips—your current customer data. Search your files and determine the average age, gender, location, income, and buying habits of your current customers (For instance, how often they make a purchase, and how many products they purchase at once). This information will help you paint the perfect picture of your target audience. Basically, you're building a profile of your perfect customer, and this tried and true profile will help you decide where to most effectively spend your marketing dollars.

Decide on Your Exclusivity Level

Now that you know who would most benefit from your products or services, it's time to make a very important decision: how exclusive you will be with your brand. How does this play into your unique selling proposition? Because some brands have made exclusivity a major part of their unique selling proposition.

For example, you probably heard about the big to-do with Abercrombie & Fitche when its CEO made the comment that the store's ideal customers were "cool, good looking people." The company says that it refuses to spend its marketing dollars on anyone outside of that group. As soon as people heard about the comment, social media was in an uproar as the people talked about how exclusionary the brand was, and a lot of people thought the store's sales would go into decline because of the comment.

But that's not what happened.

You see, the store understands who its core customer base is, and it turns out it *is* cool, good looking people. Those people stood by the store and it hasn't suffered financially as a result of the statement.

Now, this is an extreme example of what I'm talking about when I speak of exclusivity in your brand. Most of us can use the tactic to create interest in our brands and cause people, who otherwise wouldn't have been interested, to take a closer look at what we're offering.

It works like this: when people perceive a brand to be exclusive, it peaks their curiosity, and makes them want to be a part of it. It's the same concept as a marketing ploy called scarcity. When people think there is not enough of something, it makes them want it that much more. And as far as exclusivity, people are drawn to it because they figure they'll earn bragging rights about being a part of something exclusive, and that's good for your brand because it will make them want to share because they think others will view them as someone "in the know."

This was proven definitively when a new unheard of exclusive club called The 11K Club came on the scene. The premise behind it was that only 11 thousand people could sign up to get one exclusive benefit, but no one knew exactly what that benefit was. According to co-founder Steve Whyley, it was his idea of a social experiment. "I'm trying to see if people will sign up to a club they know nothing about purely because it's exclusive and because they fear they'll miss out," he says.

And they did. In fact, the owners of the club say that many more than 11 thousand people signed up for the club—all without ever knowing what it was.

How can you use exclusivity in your business? Are you an accountant who only has the capability of taking on 20 clients? Or a dog groomer who insists on meeting the dogs before agreeing to groom them to ensure that it's a good fit? You can build exclusivity into just about any brand, but before you do, make sure it will work in your situation.

Remember, when you brand your business as exclusive, by default you're going to alienate some portions of the population. It's up to you to determine whether or not the exclusivity will outweigh those losses in the long run.

What is Your Competitive Advantage?

Take a look at all of your competition and then compare them with your own business. What needs are they not meeting that you can? For instance, our landscape guy could learn that his competitors don't offer lawn care and mowing, but only the design and planting of new landscapes. He could easily step in and fill that need. Or our cupcake baker could learn that her competitors only cater to parties of more than 50 people. She could lower that number and fill the needs of moms all over the city who have smaller parties. In other words, you need to look for weak spots in your competitor's offerings and fill them. In today's business environment, you'll need to stay fresh and innovative in order to retain your market position, and looking for gaps that you can fill is one of the best ways to do it.

Here are some tips about how to identify the gaps in your marketplace.

- **Talk to your customers.** Your day-to-day customers are the best source of information you have for honing in on what the marketplace is lacking. Talk to them about their experiences with your business, and ask them for input on how it can be improved. In addition, ask them for a wish list of what products or services they would like you to offer. You'll be surprised at the insight you'll gain this way.
- **Ask your suppliers.** If you rely on industry sales representatives to keep you updated on new products and offerings, be sure to ask them about upcoming trends in the industry or shake ups with your competitors. Many of them have inside information about upcoming trends in the industry and some of them have no problem talking about other

businesses and spilling the dirt. Of course, you should keep this in mind and not tell them anything you don't want your competitors to know.

- **Go mystery shopping.** The best way to understand how your competitors are interacting with customers is to pose as one and find out firsthand. Whether you walk into their store and make a purchase, use their website, or call them to your home for a service call, evaluate every step of the process and find out how you can do it better.

This last step in the process isn't a quick task. You'll need to be slow and methodical and truly analyze each of your competitors from a customer's viewpoint.

And at the same time, you should do the same for your own business. Look at it closely from a customer's viewpoint and ask yourself what you can do better. If you're too close to the situation, ask friends and family to go through the buying process and give you an honest evaluation. The more insight you have into your customer's perceptions of both your own business and your competitors, the easier it will be for you to identify that gap and determine what your best competitive advantage is.

Make a List of Your Strongest USP Possibilities

You should now have a list of half a dozen or so possible unique selling propositions for your business. You should have pinpointed a few of your ideal customers, explored the reasons they have for buying from you, and identified what you can do better than your competitors. Now it's time to take all of that information and begin narrowing it down to come up with the perfect USP for your business.

Here's how to do it.

Your first step is to eliminate any potential USP's that won't work for some reason. For instance, if one of them highlights a benefit that your competitors are already meeting, you should eliminate that one.

Next, you'll need a visual representation for each remaining option. It doesn't have to be anything elaborate, but you should use a separate piece of paper for each option. On each piece of paper, write the rough USP statement in bold print at the top, and then create some visuals to help express it. Again, these visual don't have to be perfect because you're not going to use them, but they will get the creativity percolating in your mind. You can sketch them out or use photos or drawings from magazines.

For example, let's use our landscaper as an example. He may have a piece of paper for the following three USP's.

- Lawns from start to finish. We do it all.

- Selling your home? Increase your curb appeal with a newly landscaped yard.
- No time to do the lawn? We'll do it for you.

As you can see, these ideas aren't fleshed out, but are rough drafts of overall ideas. Now, for each idea you have, create a visual that helps express it. For example, the landscaper could draw a shiny house on a hill with a for sale sign in the perfectly manicured lawn for the second one.

Do this for each of your potential USP's. You will likely rule some of them out as you complete this exercise because it will cause you to see it with more critical eyes. Sometimes what seems like a good idea in your head just doesn't pan out when you put it to paper.

Once you have fleshed out each of your potential USP's, it's time to go to the next step.

Test Your Ideas

Hopefully you have a few ideas that you feel good about. Now it's time to put them to the test. Remember, no corporation takes an idea to market without first testing it with the types of people who would normally buy that type of product or service, and you shouldn't either. But while large corporations have huge budgets that allow them to create focus groups and do seed launches, you probably don't have that kind of budget. After all, you're just a home-based business owner, right? There's no way you can afford to test an idea before committing to it.

Think again.

Luckily, there are plenty of affordable ways for you to test your potential USP's and get real feedback from people who fit the profile of your ideal customers. Here are some ways to test your ideas:

- **Assemble a focus group.** You don't have to pay a marketing firm big bucks to assemble a focus group for you—it's easy to do yourself. Simply ask friends to ask their friends (whom you don't know) if they will be a part of the group, or place an advertisement in your local paper or on craigslist. Once the word gets out, you should have no problem convincing 5-10 people to weigh in on your potential USP's. Once assembled, pass out the sheets of paper and talk about each idea, and then ask the group for feedback. Which USP would most make them want to purchase your product or service?

- **Use an Online Focus Group.** If you're having a difficult time forming an in-person focus group, you can always form one online. Sites like Survata.com allow you create questions directed at consumers and pay between $1 and $3.50 per response, depending on how many questions you ask. Other sites like Civicom.com and insideheads.com allow you to form interactive online focus groups so you can get the feedback you need.

- **Use Social Media.** Many companies go to social media when needing consumer feedback because it's quick and easy to get people to participate. You can use sites like surveymonkey.com where you can sign up for free. Simply create a survey and use your social media accounts to get instant feedback.

- **Talk to Customers.** Let's not forget about your current customers, if you're already in business. They have unique insight into your business because, after all, they buy from you over and over again. Talk to your best customers and tell them you are creating a brand and ask them if they would provide you with some feedback. Show them your potential USP's and ask them for their opinion. They may be able to help you pinpoint exactly what you offer that keeps them coming back.

However you do it, it's vital that you get feedback from the types of people that are like your ideal customers. When you form a group or send out a survey, listen intently to the feedback you get. Some people are so attached to their ideas that they discount any feedback that isn't what they want to hear. Remember, you're asking people for their honest opinions about your marketing message—what you hear is important. After you've formed a group and listened to the feedback, you'll need to decide if you've hit the nail on the head with your USP or if you need to begin again and create a new one. Be sure to continue working on this step until you find one that resonates with consumers.

Finally, Write Your USP Statement

Now that you have chosen the USP for your brand, it's time to make it official. Do this by refining the idea and putting it into a statement that clearly shows off your brand. Imagine that our landscaper chose the first USP on his list

(Lawns from start to finish. We do it all.) His finished USP statement could look something like this:

> **We strive to be the go-to company for lawn care. We design and install beautiful landscapes, and then happily maintain them for our customers. Our customers have the most beautiful lawns on the block—without ever having to lift a finger.**

Remember, your USP is what makes your business unique, and no other competitor should be able to make the same claim. I'd like to finish this chapter by listing a few questions you should ask yourself once you've chosen your USP. If you can't answer yes to all of them, your USP isn't complete, and you should keep working on it until you can.

- Does it clearly communicate to buyers the benefits you're offering?
- Does it take the current industry trends into consideration?

- Does it represent how you want your business to be seen by the public?
- Does it convey your strongest benefit?
- Will customers remember it?
- Can you deliver on the promise?
- Does the USP specifically target your idea customer?

Whew, that was a lot of work just to build the foundation of your brand, wasn't it? But if you took each step seriously and did the required work, congratulations, you have a solid foundation for your brand that should last for years to come.

Next, we'll look at another important subject, but one that's much more fun: how to choose the right personality for your brand.

Chapter Six: Choose Your Brand's Personality

Now that you understand the very core of your brand, it's time to begin adding the elements that will make it come to life in the eyes of consumers. The first area we'll concentrate on is the personality you will attach to your brand.

What does that mean? At the root, your brand's personality is a set of human characteristics that are associated with your brand. For instance, we talked about Trader Joe's earlier and decided that it conveys a cool and hip personality.

According to research, a brand's personality is communicated to consumers in a number of ways. First, the people who represent and work in the business communicate it with their words and actions. For example, a spokesperson for a brand transfers their personality to the brand, as do the company's owner and employees when they deal with customers.

The written materials associated with the brand also convey its personality. As does the brand's identity, which is the design of the logo, marketing materials, website, social media accounts, and brand colors. So let's figure out which personality you would like to attach to your brand.

But before we delve into the personality types for brands, let's take a moment and talk about color. Many people think they should start with color when building a brand, but research shows that's just not true. Instead, studies show that a brand's color should reflect its personality in order to have the most impact on consumers. It seems that they first want to know "who" the brand is, and then see colors that reflect that personality. Those books that group colors into "meanings" and then advise people to choose a color that reflects that emotion simply don't have any science to back that up. We'll get more into the psychology of color in the next chapter, but I wanted to explain why we aren't starting there.

So let's talk about building your brand's personality.

If you've ever met someone who you considered dull or boring, then you already understand the importance of personality. And it's no different for a brand. Companies need a personality to make consumers sit up and take notice of them. Otherwise, they'll be viewed as just another company in a mass of dull sameness.

Your brand's personality should differentiate your business from the crowd and make it likeable and enduring to consumers. In other words, just as with humans, your business' personality is what will draw people to it based on the characteristics it expresses.

And how will your brand's personality reach consumers and cause them to identify with it? According to David Aaker, the undisputed expert about brand personalities, consumers will identify with your brand in one of three ways.

Through Self-Expression

According to Aaker, when people buy and use brands, it's a way of expressing either their own self, or their idealized self. For example, people who drive expensive cars make a personal statement about themselves: that they are well off and can afford to drive the car they choose. On the other hand, someone driving a truck is expressing ruggedness and an outdoorsy personality.

This carries over into any type of brand or product. Designer clothes are a great example because people use them to both express their real selves and idealized selves. For example, the well-to-do often wear designer clothes as a self-expression of who they are and what role they have in society. But people who can't really afford the clothes also wear tee-shirts with the brand's name in order to express their idealized self. It represents who they want to be—someone who can afford the clothes.

But a person doesn't have to visibly use the brand in order to use it for self-expression to occur. For example, a stay-at-home mom could be loyal to The Honest Company because she feels that it expresses who she is as a woman: environmentally conscience and natural. Even if no one sees her using the products, she feels that by using them, she is remaining true to herself.

Can you see how consumers use certain brands in order to make a personal statement? Can you shape your brand in a way that will cause people to want to use it as a form of self-expression?

As a Relationship

The second way consumers interact with brand personalities is by forming abstract "relationships" with them. These relationships are what make some consumers so loyal to their brands. Again, let's turn to Aaker for some insight. According to him, some brands conjure up the following relationship metaphors, and this causes some people to form "relationships" with the brand.

- **Someone fun to hang out with on the weekend**. A perfect example of this is beer brands. And because people like to hang out with different personality types, people will typically be loyal to the beer brand that best reflects the personality of someone they want to hang out with. For example, a blue-collar type person might want to hang out with Pabst Blue Ribbon or Budweiser because the brand personalities are casual and unpretentious, while someone who considers themselves a beer aficionado may choose to spend the weekend with Heineken, Sam Adams, or Guinness because the brands are a bit snobbish and considered upper end.
- **A trusted mom.** Some brands have personalities like moms who are loved and trusted. Some examples of this are Betty Crocker and Campbell's Soup. People loyal to these brands feel that they

can trust them and are comforted when using them.

- **A sentimental friend.** Some brands like Hallmark and Kodak take people back to their childhood with all its pleasant memories. These brands are like a well-trusted family member who evokes wonderful memories.
- **A competent and accomplished personality**. Other people are loyal to brands that have the same personalities as successful, talented people who have made something of themselves. For instance, the Wall Street Journal elicits that type of emotional response.
- **An upper crust personality.** This type of brand personality oozes wealth and power and certain types of people are fiercely loyal to it. Tiffany and Hermes are perfect examples of brands that reflect this type of personality.
- **An Outdoorsy personality.** What do Nike and The North Face have in

common? They are known for having outdoorsy and rugged personalities. These brands are followed by people who consider themselves physically fit and adventuresome.

What do you think? Can you see how forming your brand in a way that will make consumers relate to it like the above personalities can set you apart from your competitors?

Remember, these days, any brand should be designed in a way that allows for two way communication between consumers and the brand, and this is especially important in the personality portion of your brand. As you think about the above brand personality types, begin to devise some rough ideas in your head about how your "personality" could interact with your customers. For example, what would your brand say to your customers if it had to reduce it to one sentence? And what questions would your customers ask your brand?

As a Means to a Benefit

Finally, consumers can relate to a brand personality based on what benefit it promises. For instance, Volvo promises safety, and its brand personality is safe, reliable, and trustworthy. People loyal to that brand relate to that personality type and rely on the promise it makes: that it will keep them safe. Another example of a brand that does this well is Hallmark. Its personality is warm, loving, and genuine and it promises its customers an experience with those exact characteristics.

If you already own a home-based business and haven't yet created an official brand (Remember, every business has a brand whether it's intended or not), then you should first determine what your brand personality is in the eyes of your customers. The best way to do this is to ask them. Tell them that you would like to understand how they perceive your business and ask them to phrase it in human characteristics.

Now, let's delve into the personality portion of your brand a little deeper. We've talked about the ways consumers relate to a brand personality, so now let's talk about the most common human characteristics of successful brands.

The Five Core Brand Characteristics

Today's consumers have a dizzying number of choices when it comes to who they buy from, and the businesses that win are those that assign character traits to their business that make consumers "feel." These characteristics and the feelings that consumers get from them allow them to connect with a brand and build a relationship with it.

Jennifer Araker, who is a psychologist and a professor at Stanford, has studied personality in branding, and she has identified the five strongest core personality traits that can be attached to brands in her study, [Dimensions of Brand Personality](). Your brand's personality should have one of these five core characteristics as part of its personality. That's because the study surveyed 631 people about 37 different brands, and the survey subjects narrowed down and selected the most important characteristics in the brands they rated, and these five came out on top.

It only makes sense to take advantage of such a well-orchestrated survey in your own home-based business and use the results to create a top-notch brand. (Keep in mind that a small number of brands have more than one of these characteristics, but the most successful brands hone in on just one.)

Here are the top five rated brand personalities. Which one do you want to use to build your own brand?

Sincerity

A brand that comes across as sincere is able to gain the trust of consumers much easier than other brands. Why? Because when a brand is thought of as sincere, people associate these characteristics with it: honest, domestic, cheerful, and genuine. When a brand is thought of in these terms, it's easy for consumers to build a relationship with it because they trust it. Brands that make sincerity the core personality trait of their brand often find that customers not only come to trust them but are fiercely loyal.

The key to building your brand based on sincerity is to always—and I mean always—do exactly what you say you will. In other words, you have to back up your claims 100 percent and all of your actions as a business should reflect your core identity.

Want an example of a company that didn't do that and is now suffering? Whole Foods has been thought of for years as a company dedicated to only selling healthy foods that its customers could trust. It got into trouble recently when it came out that the store is loaded with foods made from GMO's. That was bad news for the company because emblazed across the front of some of its stores is the slogan "Nothing Artificial Ever."

Its customers were outraged when they discovered that they'd been lied to. As a result, many of its former customers are boycotting the store and the press has continually written articles about the deception. As a result, Whole Foods is experiencing a serious sales slowdown.

What can you learn from this brand disaster? Keep your promises. Whatever you decide for your USP, make sure that you can back it up. And for goodness sake, if you plan to use sincerity as your brand's personality trait, keep it real.

This is important because a study was conducted that measured what happened when businesses using a sincerity personality did something bad, but unintentional, in customer's eyes. The study showed that brands that were thought of as sincere had a much more difficult time recuperating than other brands after a misstep. The study showed that up until the point that the brand made the error, customer loyalty was strong, but afterwards, even though the brand apologized and tried to make up for it, its customers showed a lack of trust.

And finally, remember that just because you have a great theme for your sincerity brand, that doesn't mean consumers will believe it. For example, your message may be based on love, friendship or the local community, but if your intentions and actions don't back that up, they'll see right through it.

One of the best ways to determine whether or not your brand is right for a sincerity personality is to ask yourself these three questions:

- **Is your USP true?** I hope your answer is yes, but if you have doubts that you can back it up, you should not use sincerity as your brand personality. (You should also revise it because having a USP that isn't true is a sure way to fail.)
- **Will it cause you to weaken your position?** Many entrepreneurs mistake a sincere brand for a wimpy one, but

that's not the case. You can have a rugged or in-your-face brand and still use sincerity as your brand personality. But if you don't get that brands are multi-dimensional and are tempted to water down your brand when using sincerity, it may not be the right personality for you.

- **Can you carry it through to social media?** Using social media the right way will play an integral part of establishing and promoting your brand, and if you don't think you can relay the sincerity message properly on your channels, you should think about another brand personality.

So, what's the takeaway for using a sincerity brand? Do what you say you're going to do, don't lie to your customers, and give them a reason to trust you.

Competence

Brands that portray competence as their personality are thought of as responsible, reliable, efficient, and dependable. But studies have shown that in order to make a competence brand successful, it needs to be paired with warmth.

Just as people size each other up to determine each other's intentions, consumers look at brands the same say. And in order for a brand to successfully use a competence personality, it must first exhibit warmth. Let's sum it up this way: when consumers perceive a brand as warm, it means they trust that the brand has their best interests at heart. Once that's been established, consumers will look for competence to determine whether the brand can deliver.

Perhaps the best description of this phenomenon was related by Chris Malone and Susan T. Fiske in the book, *The Human Brand*. They use the television show *Survivor* as a comparison to show the importance of using both warmth and competence together when branding a business.

They say that, just as with humans, if a brand exhibits warmth without competence, people will feel pity or sympathy for them. But if a brand exudes competence without warmth, it makes people suspicious of it. And if a brand shows neither of the human characteristics, it draws disgust and contempt.

A perfect example of a company that exemplifies this is Costco. It's perceived as warm because it takes the stance that if it treats its employees well, they will deliver excellent customer service to its customers. And it's considered competent because makes good on its promises.

On the other hand, Lululemon is an example of an epic failure of this type of branding. Until 2013, the company experienced a huge success and fiercely loyal customers. But then they sold some yoga pants that were see through and when customers tried to return them, they weren't treated with warmth. In fact, there were rumors that store employees were requiring women to bend over to prove the pants were see through.

Customers who were used to being treated warmly by a competent company responded with rage and the store, which had been wildly successful, experienced a $60 million loss of revenues.

This leads us to our next point. According to Malone and Fiske, you must be able to do three things if you want to use warmth and competence for your business branding. Whether you currently run a home-based business or you're just getting started, these exercises can help you create a competence brand that works.

- **Be self-aware**. It's not enough to think that consumers consider your brand to be warm and competent. Instead, you should constantly survey them and measure their perceptions of your brand. One way to do this is to use the free tool at LoyaltyTest.com to elicit customer opinions about your brand. In addition, keep the conversation open with your customers and continually ask for feedback as to how they perceive your business.

- **React to the feedback**. It's important to listen to the feedback, and if necessary, use it to make changes so that consumer perception matches your desired brand personality. Even if you believe that the feedback is wrong, remember that your goal is to please your customers so you should be open to their opinions and willing to make adjustments.
- **Put the customer first**. You've heard it a thousand times, but it's easy to forget when you're concentrating on employees, profits and marketing. But in order to come across as a warm and competent brand, you will always have to put the customer first. If you can't do this, you should consider a different brand personality.

Just like with sincerity, a brand that exhibits warmth and competency will quickly develop a following of loyal customers. But if you're leaning toward this type of brand personality, it's imperative that you develop it slowly and steadily, always keeping your customers at the forefront of your mind.

Excitement

Brands that use excitement as their personality are considered daring, spirited, imaginative, and up-to-date. These brands have the ability to build excitement in customers and make them see the possibilities. Many brands who use this personality type are young and hip, but even established brands have been known to use it.

For example, a few years ago, Pepsi realized that it needed to update its brand and after a lot of testing and thought, settled on an excitement personality. It created a new tagline, "Live for Now" to go with the new persona. A spokesman for the company explained that while its rival

Coke "represents happiness and moments of joy, while it protects culture and maintains the status quo," Pepsi "creates culture and embraces individuality." He claims that people who love Pepsi think that "leading an exciting life is much more important than leading a happy one." (Do you see how Pepsi knew who its ideal customer was before creating its new brand personality?)

One of my favorite young and hip brands that use this personality is Johnny Cupcakes, the world's first t-shirt bakery. Talk about inventive! The owner, Johnny Earle, was in a rock band and given the nickname of Johnny Cupcake. He designed a t-shirt for it with a cupcake with crossbones on the front. The t-shirt attracted attention and he soon began making them and selling them out of the trunk of his car. The business grew so quickly that he opened a t-shirt store, but it wasn't like any the world has ever seen.

The store is built to look like a bakery and the t-shirts are displayed in bakery cases and baking pans. The owner says that he set out to create a t-shirt store like no other, and he definitely accomplished it. This brand brilliantly uses an excitement personality type and has seen great success with it. In addition, his story, which is prominently displayed at Johnnycupcakes.com is laid out in chapter form and contributes to the excitement of the brand.

Companies that use the excitement brand personality need to approach the process with a little more gusto. In fact, building a brand based on excitement will require you to excel in the following areas:

- **Social media.** While social media plays a vital role in all brand personalities, those businesses that have an excitement personality have to approach it in a more innovative way. For instance, the owner of Johnny Cupcakes has been known to use social media to ask fans to show up at a certain ice cream shop with their

Johnny Cupcakes t-shirt on in exchange for a free ice cream.

- **Trends.** Brands that rely on excitement also have to keep up with the most current trends in order to stay relevant and up-to-date. Customers who are loyal to these brands rely on them to keep them current about trends and happenings, and that helps fuel the excitement of the brand.
- **Innovate.** Finally, excitement brands must constantly innovate in order to keep things exciting. Once a brand using this type of personality stops innovating and becomes stale, they will no longer be able to live up to the promise of their brand.

In short, if you want to build an excitement brand, you'll need to be seen as cutting edge, relevant, and trendsetting by consumers.

Ruggedness

Our fourth brand personality type is ruggedness. In this type of brand personality, a company's product or service is perceived as strong, outdoorsy, rugged, and tough. The idea behind this type of personality is that customers will see your business (or products) as unbreakable and strong.

One of the most memorable rugged brands in history is the Marlboro Man. The concept was born in the 50's when the company needed to find a way to appeal to men. You see, Marlboro was a filtered cigarette, and up until that time, those types of cigarettes were thought of as feminine. So the advertising executives came up with the Marlboro Man in order to appeal to men. And boy did it work. The cigarette quickly became known as a cigarette for men because of the rugged persona the brand displayed.

You can see the ruggedness personality conveyed by plenty of brands these days, such as REI, Ford, Kitchen Aid, and even a community in British Columbia called Lillooet, which advertises with the tagline, "Guaranteed Rugged."

As you can see from the above list, a rugged brand doesn't necessarily only appeal to men, although many times it does. A perfect example of this is the newest branding of Old Spice. The company is staying true to its rugged and masculine brand, but is now appealing to women with its "Man Your Man Could Smell Like" campaign.

In the [commercials](#), an attractive actor is seen wearing only a bath towel and opens with the line, "Hello ladies." He goes on to tell the audience that if they would only buy their man Old Spice, they would smell like him. The spot features him going from the bathroom to a yacht, to riding a horse. It's a perfect example of a rugged brand that appeals to women and men alike.

The key to building a rugged brand is to emphasize functionality over showiness. You'll need to identify the core benefit of your brand

and promote it with this personality. Just remember, you still want consumers to find your brand attractive, but its ruggedness should be the highlight.

Sophistication

Finally, some brands use sophistication as their personality, but of all the five brand personalities, this is the most difficult to achieve. Some of the most well-known brands that rely on sophistication are Vango Art, Tiffany, and Versace. A sophisticated brand is ultra-premium and upper class. These brands are charming, glamorous, and romantic and they seek to inspire and uplift their customers.

Building a brand with a sophistication personality takes time and if this is your desire, you'll need to look at it as a long game. For instance, some sophisticated brands took a decade or more to establish.

If this is the type of brand personality you want to use for your business, you'll need to constantly reinforce your brand in order to appeal to luxury consumers. For example, if you run a home-based interior design business and only want to cater to high end clients, you'll need to convey your sophisticated brand with all your social media channels and the marketing pieces that make up your identity on a regular, repeated basis. For instance, you could start a campaign that encourages customers to share their experiences with your brand, or talk about why they prefer to use it over less expensive alternatives. In order to achieve success, you would run this campaign for a long period of time, if not indefinitely.

The feel you should attempt to create is aspirational luxury. In other words, market your brand in a way that makes consumers aspire to what you have to offer. Remember, brand personality is emotional and this personality in particular should inspire strong emotions associated with your brand.

Now that we've covered the five most common and useful brand personalities, I can just hear some of you asking what to do if your brand is boring and you don't think you can do anything to make it exciting enough for customers to notice.

Let's address that now because honestly, some home-based business owners are faced with that exact problem.

How Build a Brand if Your Product or Service is Boring

Let's face it, a home-based accounting business, cleaning service, or a tree trimming business doesn't automatically inspire excitement does it? If you run a business that you think is boring or doesn't lend itself to an exciting or motivational brand, I want you to consider something: toilet paper.

Toilet paper? Yep.

Let me tell you what the geniuses behind Charmin toilet paper did, and then we'll talk about your own boring brand. Because really, it's difficult to find a product more boring than toilet paper, isn't it?

In 2014, the Charmin launched a twitter campaign using the hashtag #tweetfromtheseat. It urged people to tweet poems, inspirational quotes and even their own poems, writings, and music from, well, the seat. The campaign was a huge success and this excitement based personality branding was a huge hit. All it took was a little imagination and a platform for consumers to interact with each other and the brand.

Need some more inspiration? Let's think about razors. Can anyone forget the instantly viral YouTube video that Dollar Shave Club put out a few years ago? People all over the world watched it time and time, and get this, it was about *razors*.

So, what does that have to do with your boring home-based business? You can learn a lot from these branding examples and apply it to your own business. Here are the takeaways:

- **Humor works.** If you can take a boring product or service and use humor to connect with consumers, you'll stand out from the crowd. But the key is to make the humor relate to your brand. For example, in the Dollar Shave Club video, the company didn't take itself too seriously or try to make razors more important than they are, and as a result, the humor hit just the right cord with the public.
- **Be authentic.** When Charmin started the #tweetfromtheseat hashtag, it stayed 100 percent true to the brand. It didn't try to reinvent itself to make the brand cooler or more acceptable, it just stayed true to what it is and gave customers something to laugh about for what is typically thought of as a boring brand.

- **Do the unexpected.** Think your brand is boring? What about insurance? Can it get any more snooze worthy? When Allstate was faced with rebranding their boring insurance business, they hit it big with the [Mayhem](#) (excitement) personality. The company shook things up in the industry by using this personality to point out everything that can go wrong, but making the point that whatever it is, the brand has you covered.

The common theme in all of these branding examples is that businesses with dull brands used humor to create excitement for their brand. If you run a business with a product that is considered boring or dull, can you use a little humor with your brand's personality to liven things up a little?

So, what do you think? Does one of these personality types stand out in your mind for your business? If so, are the wheels turning about how you can use that personality to connect with consumers and make them loyal to your brand?

If so, great! But don't stop reading and begin devising your brand just yet because we've got more ground to cover, and in order to create the best brand for your business, you'll need some more information before you begin building.

Next, I'd like to talk about how to successfully use colors in your brand. Get your creative hat on because you'll need it for the next chapter.

Chapter Seven: How Colors Affect Your Brand's Success or Failure

There is a lot of bad information out there in regards to how colors should be used in brands. If you surf the internet, you'll be inundated with people telling you that you should choose a color because it will make consumers do or feel something. But when you look at the research, especially the research regarding branding, you'll quickly realize that all those words aren't backed up by research and science.

I mentioned in the last chapter that studies show choosing a color without first understanding your brand's personality is an exercise in futility. That's because consumers want to see a color that's based on a brand's personality, otherwise the entire picture of the brand won't make sense to them.

Let's me give you an example to drive home the point. Imagine that our landscape guy wanted to create a sincerity personality because he wanted trust to be at the core of his USP. So he created a brand that used a photo of himself along with a tagline that promised customers they could count on him to show up and do a good job. Now, this landscaper read an article that said the color red made people buy things, so he used that color for his logo. Can you image people's confusion when they saw his advertisement?

It's a perfect example of someone choosing a color with no relation to their USP or brand personality. (Red is typically associated with excitement, not trust.) The landscaper would have done better to choose green or blue, both of which would have been a perfect extension of his brand personality.

Now, I'm not saying that there is no psychology behind certain colors—there is. But how we use them in branding is different than how the world at large uses them. Rather than use a color based on stereotypical color associations, you should to use them to cause customers to perceive your business and brand as you want them to. In short, consumers expect a brand's color to fit what the business is selling.

For example, many color experts will tell you that using the color green will cause your customers to be calm and peaceful. Tell that to the John Deere Tractors brand where green is prominent in its logo and marketing materials. The tractor company is a rugged brand personality, and the color green still fits its message perfectly.

But now that you have thought about what your USP and brand personality might be, let's take a good look at color psychology—in the context of branding—to determine which colors are right for your brand.

The General Psychology of Colors

While it's true that there is no magic chart that will tell you which color to use that will elicit the consumer response you want, there are some general guidelines that you should *take into consideration* because they generally align with specific traits. For example, in the broadest of terms, purple is aligned with sophistication, red with excitement, and brown is often thought of as rugged. But these are just general guidelines because brands use these colors to express different traits and have great success with them. For example, Taco Bell uses purple, which is usually thought of sophisticated.

Here is a rundown of the main brand colors and the general guidelines for their use in branding.

Red

Red is an attention getting color that is considered passionate, loud, warm, active and angry, with hints of danger. Scientists have proven that just seeing the color red makes people's heart rate and blood pressure go up.

As consumers, we've been trained that when we see the color red in stop signs, danger signs or red lights, we need to stop what we're doing, and that's the action companies hope for when using this color for their brand. Companies like Netflix, Target, Coca Cola and Wendy's all use the color and hope that it causes consumers to stop what they're doing and take the next step. (Which is to buy their product.) The theory is that red causes consumers to believe that they need a product right away.

In addition, the theory is that red also makes people hungry, which is why so many fast food restaurants use it in their logo and signage. The color is a boost for fast food restaurants because being an activity color, it makes people want to eat quickly and leave, which is what the restaurants want them to do.

If you want a picture of a brand using colors wisely, look at McDonalds. It uses red and yellow in its restaurants to make people hungry and anxious to eat and leave in a hurry. But it wants people to linger on its website, so it tones down the red and yellow and instead uses a soothing combination of soft grays, blues, rose and black. Smart, isn't it?

Excitement brand personalities do well with red.

Orange

Orange is considered a creative and playful color that brings about fun, energy, activity, brightness, friendliness, and spunk. On the other hand, orange can also mean caution so brands that use it have to do so carefully.

Many companies that use it hope to convey playfulness, a sense of fun and encourage creativity and action in consumers. Some of the brands that use this color are The Home Depot, Fanta, Nickelodeon, Gatorade, and many sports teams.

One word of caution about orange—used correctly it will make your business stand out, but if you overuse it and overwhelm customers, they may be turned off by it. People tend to either love or hate the color, so much thought and consideration should go into using this color for your brand.

Excitement brand personalities also do well with this color.

Yellow

Yellow has been proven to catch consumer's eyes faster than other colors, and that's why many brands use it as a secondary color in addition to a primary one. But a few brave companies are brave enough to use the optimistic, bright, and eye-catching color as the main focus. The color is said to inspire optimism, happiness, joy, energy, imagination, respect—and it makes people smile.

Brands that use yellow are McDonalds, Subway and Best Buy, which all focus on creating a happy space for customers. On the other hand, Caterpillar, the construction equipment manufacturer, also uses the color to great success.

The key to using yellow is to use it sparingly. Studies have shown that too much of the color can cause consumers to lose focus or become argumentative.

What type of brand personality does well with yellow? You guessed it—excitement.

Pink

The color pink has the ability to evoke strong emotions, but what those emotions are depends of the shade of pink that's used. For instance, a soft, pale pink makes people feel relaxed, calm, and reminiscent of childhood memories. Brands like Victoria's Secret, Barbie, Baskin Robbins, and Mary Kay all use the color. These companies primarily market to women and they play up the gender-based color with their brand.

On the other hand, some companies use a stronger shade of pink that can also appeal to men. For instance, T-Mobile uses a magenta pink in its logo and markets to both men and women.

Using the color pink when you're marketing to women is smart because it immediately pinpoints you as a feminine company, but some brands, like T-Mobile took a chance by using the color to stand out from the crowd, and it paid off.

Depending on the shade of pink you choose, a sophisticated, sincere, or excitement personality would do well with this color.

Purple

The color purple allow creates different feelings in people, depending on whether it's pale or dark. Pale lavender typically makes people feel sentimental and nostalgic, while a deeper purple is often associated with royalty or sophistication. It's said be able to calm nerves, uplift people, and encourage creativity.

This color is a bit ambiguous, which means that it can easily adapt into a variety of meanings and emotions of brands. This makes it the color of choice for experimental brands, or those that want to stand out and forge their own way. Some of the brands that use this versatile color are Taco Bell, Yahoo! And Monster.com.

Any brand personality would do well using purple because it's such an ambiguous color, but sophistication is an obvious choice because of its association with royalty.

Green

Green is one of the most adaptable colors in the spectrum. It's considered a positive color that conveys growth, rebirth, and nature. And depending on which shade of green is used, it can also signify abundance, prosperity, wealth, and luxury or endurance and stability. A dark forest green is manly and traditional, while a lime green is considered refreshing and peaceful. Green is also associated with brands that have to do with nature or organics.

Do you see what I mean?

Brands as diverse as Spotify, H & R Block, Animal Planet, and Starbucks all rely on green for their primary color, although in different shades.

Green can be used as the main color in a brand, but even if you want to use a primary color such as yellow or red, the addition of green as a secondary color will help balance it out.

Rugged, sincere, and competent brands are all personalities that should consider green for their color.

Blue

One of the most commonly used colors, blue is known for being calming, reassuring, peaceful, orderly, and causing people to trust a brand. Brands that use this color are seen as dependable, trustworthy, and stress-free.

Many airlines, such as Continental, use blue as a way of calming its passengers. And financial corporations such as American Express also use the color to build trust. In addition, Walmart uses the color blue to express reliability and order.

If you are considering using a sincerity brand, blue would be a great choice for your color. In addition, a competent brand would benefit from using this color.

Brown

Brown is another color that is earthy in feel and goes well with brands who are somehow related to nature. The traits associated with this color are efficiency, reliability, simplicity, honesty, and dependability. The brands that use this color typically want to get across that they are good at what they do and can be trusted—without all of the fanfare of brands that use colors like red and yellow.

For example, USP uses brown and is thought of as a company that does its job without making a big fuss about it. They get in, they do the job, and they leave. It's what their good at, and that's why people trust them.

If you plan to use sincerity, competence, or ruggedness as your brand personality, brown might be the right color for you.

Black

Not many companies use black as their primary branding color, but those that do make a powerful statement. The color is typically used to portray confidence and sophistication. Companies like Ralph Lauren's Polo Black and Guinness use black to convey mystery, sophistication, and depth.

If your brand personality is sophistication, you might consider making a bold statement by using black as your primary color.

White

On the other hand, white is typically used as a primary color to convey innocence, simplicity, openness, and creativity. Perhaps the best example of a brand using white is Apple. Healthcare and baby brands also make use of this color.

You should consider white as your primary color if your brand personality is sophisticated or sincere.

Who would have thought the color you choose for your brand could have so many implications? That's why it's so important for you to have a thorough understanding of what your company is and what it stands for before ever thinking about which colors you'll use for your brand. Remember, [studies](#) show that consumers want to see that a brand's colors match its personality, not the other way around.

When a brand's colors are in line with its personality, it becomes believable in the minds of consumers. But when they're off, the brand can look fake or contrived. That's why it's important to choose your color based on your brand's personality, no matter how much you want to use a different color. Ask yourself how consumers will feel looking at the whole of your brand. Will they see it as a cohesive brand that makes sense, or simply a jumble of personality and colors that are confusing?

Finally, if you want to see the exact color schemes of the world's most successful brands, head on over to brandcolors.net. There, you'll see a listing of hundreds of brands with the color schemes they use. You can learn a lot from this site, and even use it to help develop your own brand colors based on examples of successful brands.

Before we move on to the next topic, I'd like to leave you with a few facts that you should consider for your brand's color.

- Blue is the favorite color of most men and women.
- Many women love purple, but not many men list it as a favorite color.
- Men prefer bold colors, while women prefer softer colors.
- [Research](#) shows that new brands should differentiate themselves by choosing colors that are different from their established competitors.
- Let me say it again, [research](#) clearly shows that choosing your colors based on the appropriateness to the brand's personality is more important than the color itself in consumer's eyes.

Okay, are you ready to move on? Next, we're going to tap into your creative side to begin thinking about your brand's identity. What is that? Let's go to the next chapter to find out.

Chapter Eight: How to Create Your Brand's Identity with Logos, Taglines and More

We're moving along pretty good, aren't we? You've learned that the first thing you have to do when branding your home-based business is to define what makes you different from your competitors. This is called your unique selling proposition, and you'll most likely identity it by looking for a gap in your marketplace that others aren't filling. Next, you'll need to decide what type of personality you want your brand to convey. I've given you a list of the five personalities that are the most successful in the eyes of consumers. Once you've decided on your brand's personality, you'll need to choose a color that best identifies with that type of personality in order for consumers to "believe" your brand.

Now comes the next part: creating your brand's identity.

Let's start by defining what that is.

What is a Brand Identity?

It's easy to get brand personality and brand identify mixed up, but they are very different concepts that work differently to boost your brand in the eyes of customers. As we've discussed, brand personality is a combination of human traits that best reflect the brand. It is based on emotions, and it's what causes consumers to become attached to a brand.

Brand identity is the make-up of the external factors you use to relate to and communicate with consumers. It is made up of all the communications and visuals that you'll begin thinking about in this chapter. For instance, your brand identity will be based on your logo, brand story, fonts, colors, and all your communications. It should coordinate and play off of your brand personality. For example, if you've decided on an excitement personality, you'll want your identity to match it. If it doesn't and you instead use somber colors and images, the brand wouldn't appear authentic to your consumers and it will leave them confused.

Here is a brief overview of the differences between brand personality and brand identity to drive home the point even more:

- A brand personality is based on how your business speaks and the actions it takes. The identity is based on the external communications associated with the brand—both functional and mental.
- Brand personality is made up of human characteristics, while brand identity is the visual images that are an extension of those characteristics.
- Brand personality is a long-term effort that will last for years, while your identity should be forward looking. It's what the brand aspires to.
- Brand personality is made up of consumer experiences with your

company, while your identity is made up of all that you do for your customers.

Does that make it clearer? I hope so, because now it's time for you to begin forming your brand's identity.

But first, I'd like to clear something up. Earlier in the book, I advised you to read a few chapters before you begin to create and define your brand. We've now covered the chapters that I felt necessary in order for you begin working on your brand. You now have the basics, and in fact, should construct at least a rough idea of your brand's USP, personality and colors before attempting to create its identity.

At the same time, if you want to simply continue reading and then build your brand after you've finished the book that's fine, too. I just want to make sure that you construct your brand in the order I've laid out so you'll have the best chance for success.

Okay, are you ready to begin constructing your brand's identity? Let's start with your story.

Creating Your Brand's Story

Seth Godwin, entrepreneurial expert extraordinaire, says, "Marketing is no longer about the stuff that you make, but about the stories you tell."

And he's right. In today's marketplace, it's no longer enough to tell customers how great your product or service is, you have to show them. And because today's consumers want to connect with brands, stories are the best way to do that.

Now that you know what personality you want your brand to convey, you'll need to create a story that will make the personality ring true. Let me give you an example so you'll understand just how critical this is.

I want you to remember the last time you met someone new and really connected with them. In all likelihood, you forged a friendship because you shared the same values, had a great time talking about past experiences, and maybe even told a joke or two. In other words, you connected because of personality.

It's no different for brands and consumers. A brand's personality is what draws consumers to it and helps build a relationship. And what's behind a personality? A story.

When you begin thinking about your brand's story—which will connect your brand and consumers—there is one thing you should keep in mind: it must be unique. Now I realize that just about every type of story that can be told has already been done, but it doesn't matter. In order for your story to get attention and resonate with consumers, you'll have to put a unique spin on it and make it better—much better—than your competitor's story.

Let's look to a brand that so uniquely told their "average" story it instantly became a viral success. That brand is Chipotle.

A few years ago, the brand released a video titled [The Scarecrow](), and it sums up Chipotle's story better than anything else they could have done. The Mexican food chain is known for healthy Mexican food that uses fresher ingredients, and in this video the character, who is a Scarecrow, is employed by a fast food chain that puts out unhealthy, unnatural food. The people at the receiving end of it don't know how unhealthy it is because they simply receive their meal in a box. This makes the scarecrow sad and he begins to think there has to be a better way.

In the end, Scarecrow uses fresh ingredients from his own garden to serve people real food that is fresh and healthy. And that's Chipotle's story: a Mexican food restaurant in a sea of others that does things differently and healthier.

But that story has been told a thousand times, right? A business that claims to do things better than all of its competitors? Yes, and Chipotle knew that, which is why it told the story in a unique way that no one else had ever done before.

Which brings us to your story. Using your USP, you'll need to create a story that is entertaining, while educating consumers on the benefits of doing business with you. For example, in Chipotle's story, the video clearly shows the difference between eating at a regular fast food place and its store. The video elicits a wide variety of emotions, and convinces viewers that if they're going to eat fast food, it had better be Chipotle. If you haven't already watched it, I urge you to click the link above. (Or if you're reading this in hardcover, search for "The Scarecrow/Chipotle" on YouTube.

Your story doesn't have to be fiction, like in the case of Chipotle. It can be your actual story and tell consumers how you came to be in business.

Was it a lifelong dream fulfilled, a desire to fill a need, or is your business an active part of the community and that's what makes it special?

Regardless of whether your story is fictional or based on real life, you'll need to include certain elements in it so consumers will connect with your brand. What are those elements? I'm glad you asked.

- **Emotion.** This is perhaps the most important aspect of your story because it's what will allow consumers to connect with your brand. Your story needs to make consumers *feel*, and that will draw them to your brand. For example, in Chipotle's "The Scarecrow," what feelings did the story arouse in you? If you're like most people, you were rooting for Scarecrow, you felt sorry for the people who were eating the unhealthy boxed meals, you were a little angry at what passes for food these days, you were excited when Scarecrow came up with the idea for fresh food, and you were thrilled when he began selling it. Keep in mind that Chipotle never even hinted at selling its products to viewers. It simply had a story to tell, and that story led consumers to the brand. How can you write your story in a way that will make consumers feel?

- **Passion.** In addition to making consumers feel, you've got to make it obvious that you're passionate about your brand. When consumers feel your passion, it's contagious and they're more likely to share it with their friends.
- **Sincerity.** You not only have to be passionate about your story, but also sincere. If consumers don't believe that you're sincere when you tell your story, they won't believe in or connect with your brand. What does it feel like when a story is sincere? After watching "The Scarecrow," did you doubt for even one

moment that Chipotle cares are fresh food?

- **Engagement.** One of your chief goals for creating a great story for your brand is to cause consumers to engage with it. Remember this as you create your own story. When consumers saw "The Scarecrow," millions of them watched it on YouTube (over 5.5 million within days of it releasing, and over 16 million since then), and then countless viewers shared the video on their social media accounts. Conversations were happening all over the world about what real food looks like. How can you get your local community talking, or if you run an online store, your global customers? Modcloth, an online vintage clothing retailer based in San Francisco, created a YouTube channel and then used it to offer lessons and contests in order to engage its users. And it worked—thousands of people watch their videos and click through to their website. Remember, your home-based business is part of a community, and while your goal may not be to get the entire world talking about your story, you should strive to get those in your local area excited about it.

In addition to these four elements, your story will need to contain certain storyline and timeline elements in order to hit home with consumers. Here is a basic outline of a well-written brand story, and the necessary elements that make it good.

- **A character.** Depending on your story, your main character could be you, a customer, or a spokesperson or mascot. The key is that the character in your story is relatable so consumers will be able to connect to them and care about what happens to them. Chipotle's Scarecrow worked because it was sad about something it felt was important, and decided to take steps to change it—something everyone has experienced.

- **Imagery.** Whether you're telling your brand story on YouTube, your social media channels, or in printed materials, you'll need some imagery to help people visualize it. Use photos, graphs, videos, infographics, and descriptive language to help consumers experience your story more fully.
- **A problem.** Your character should be facing a problem that must be solved or overcome, and the stakes should be very clear to the reader, viewer, or listener. For instance, the Scarecrow's problem was unhealthy food, and the video shows countless unsuspecting people eating it, likely putting their health at risk. But viewers got to watch him overcome it by starting a business that sold fresh food. Your problem could be the main issue your customers face, and in a subtle way (without selling) you could show how

your product or service could help them overcome it. Or you could take a cue from Chipotle and show the problem you faced that led you to open the business.

- **Pursuit.** The story shouldn't only revolve around what the character is experiencing, but in order for consumers to connect with it, it should also focus on what the character is *doing*. Is he pursuing a lofty goal? Battling an impossible situation? Trying to enact justice where there is none?

- **Progression.** Remember, every story has a beginning, where the premise of the story is set up, a middle where the main conflict is shown, and an end, where the problem is solved. This is true whether you're creating a video like Chipotle did, or writing your company's story for your website. Be sure to gently lead the viewer to the realization that your brand can solve the problem, but don't do it in a salsey way or they will write it off as simply another promotional piece. Remember, if your story is interesting enough and impactful, you don't have to sell them because people will take action on their own.

- **Surprise.** One way to make your story stand out from the crowd is by throwing in something unexpected that surprises your audience. This could be a twist in the story, or an unexpected ending.
- **Open Ended.** Rather than telling the audience what it should think at the end of your story, you should allow them to draw their own conclusions. Otherwise, you take away the enjoyment of them discovering the message for themselves and sharing it. For example, The Scarecrow never preached about the importance of healthy food, but viewers walked away understanding the message.
- **Language.** You should speak to your ideal customer in a language that they will understand. Don't use big words or

drawn out sentences to impress them, but rather speak to them as you would a friend.

- **Resolution**. At the end of the story, the consumer should feel satisfied because there was a resolution. This can be when the character overcomes the problem, or in your personal story, when you first opened your doors. Whatever you use, the consumer should walk away uplifted and satisfied.

You may not use all of these elements in your brand story, but you should strive to use as many of them as you can. I know most of you aren't writers, and the thought of creating such an important story makes you wish you'd never read this chapter, but trust me, it will be well worth it.

But if just don't know where to start, you can always use a classic story pattern. These story patterns are the backbone of many successful stories, and when you use your own details to make it personal, it will come to life. Here are a few classic story patterns you can base your brand story on.

- The hero's journey
- A triumph of a personal nature
- A guru that gives someone guidance
- An adventure, journey or quest
- A coming-of-age story
- A story that revolves around history

Finally, if you're truly challenged in this department, you can always hire a professional to do it for you. I would recommend listing a job posting on UpWork to look for a professional writer. But here's a word of caution—don't hire someone who has never done this before. Instead look for a writer who has experience in writing brand stories. You can do this by typing "brand story" into the UpWork search box, and then checking the portfolio of each freelancer that comes up.

Now that you understand how important your brand story is, and how to write one, let's move on to something else: your tagline.

What is a Brand Tagline?

A brand tagline only consists of a few words, but creating it may be the most difficult thing you'll do when designing your brand. Why? Because you'll have to whittle down your USP to five words or less. AND those words have to be so memorable and unique that consumers will have a hard time forgetting them.

Remember, your brand identity is the visual expression of your brand, and that includes the logo and tagline. The logo is the graphic representation of your brand, and the tagline is a short statement that succinctly sums up your biggest benefit, distinction, or advantage a customer has when doing business with you. In other words, it's your USP narrowed down to a few words. The tagline is often seen with the logo, or in many cases, is a part of it.

So, why are we not talking about how to design your logo first? Because I believe if you spend some time creating your tagline, you will be better equipped to design your logo. Taglines are incredibly difficult, but the act of doing it will likely spur some creativity for your logo. That's because it will force you think about your USP and how to clearly define and express it.

Let me give you some examples of famous taglines so you can understand what you're shooting for. Who wants you to "Just do it"? Which brand lets you "Have it your way?" And quick—what "Melts in your mouth, not in your hands?"

If you answered Nike, Burger King, and M&Ms, then you've been on the receiving end of these brand's marketing messages.

But exactly what goes into the making of such a memorable tagline, and how can you create one for your own business? Let's start by talking about what each of these taglines, and all other successful taglines, have in common.

- **It's unique**. A tagline that is so unique to a brand that it couldn't possibly be attached to another brand is one characteristic that successful taglines share. It is a part of the brand, and consumers can't imagine the brand operating without it.
- **It stands on its own.** Did you need to see the Nike swoosh when you read "Just do it," or did the tagline stand on its own? Being recognizable with or without the logo is another characteristic of a successful tagline.
- **It's sticky.** Great taglines are sticky, and consumers have a difficult time getting them out of their head.
- **It's everywhere.** One of the reasons you recognize the taglines so easily is because the brands use them in every advertising and marketing effort they

make. Once you create a great tagline, it should become a permanent part of your brand—in everything you do.

Now that you know the common characteristics of a successful tagline, let's talk about how to create one. There are some specific steps you'll need to take to create a perfect tagline for your brand.

Start with Some Inspiration

If you're like most people, you need a little something to kick your brain into action when doing a daunting task such as this. Luckily, there are some free tagline generators that will help you get started. Keep in mind that I would **never** recommend you use the taglines these computer programs spit out, but you might see something that inspires you to create the perfect one. Go to Sloganizer.net, SloganGenerator.co, and Procato.com to kick off your brainstorming session.

Think About Your USP

You remember that don't you? The one thing that makes you different than the competition and gives your customers a key benefit when they buy from you? Your tagline will need to be based on that, so get it straight in your mind and begin thinking about short phrases that apply—and be sure to make the message something your customers care about. Your end result should be five words or less, so try to keep your rough drafts as short as you can get them. Start jotting down catchy phrases that point out your USP.

Remember that your tagline doesn't have to be clever, but it does need to clearly convey your USP to consumers in a way that they instantly understand. If someone saw your tagline on your website or your business card, they should instantly understand what your business stands for and offers.

Now Make it Yours

Now that you have a few rough drafts, begin playing with the words until you create something unique. You could twist a common phrase to make it your own or use rhythms or word plays. Keep playing with it until you're happy with it.

Speak it Out Loud

If you create something you like, don't just keep it on paper. Say the tagline out loud to make sure it's easy to say and rolls off the tongue. Ask your friends, family and customers to do the same and then ask for feedback.

Set it Aside

Once you've created your brand's tagline, you'll need to set it aside until you've designed your logo. Your tagline will either be a part of your logo or displayed alongside it every time it appears.

Once again, if you get stuck and want a professional to create your tagline, you should look to UpWork and find a freelancer with experience in this area. But remember, no one knows your business like you do, and so you should make every effort to at least do the rough drafts before hiring someone else to do it so they'll understand the direction you want to take.

Ready for the next item in your brand's identity? Let's move on and learn how to create a logo that consumers will remember.

How to Create a Brand Logo that Resonates with Consumers

Now we've come to the last aspect of your visual brand—the logo. Although tiny in size, your logo is vitally important. It's the face of your business, and must convey the benefits you offer to consumers, the brand's promise, and a concise expression of your brand's personality.

All of that in a simple logo? Yep.

Let's take a look at a couple of well-known logos that do it brilliantly.

I don't even have to tell you which company this logo belongs to, do I? Apple's logo is universally known, but it's what it portrays that I would like to look at today. On the surface, the apple is missing a "byte," which gives it deeper meaning, but it conveys more than that. Apple is known for clean lines and simplicity in design, and its label makes that promise to consumers by the mere simplicity of it.

Let's take a look at another one to even further drive home the point.

amazon.com

Amazon is another brand that uses simplicity in its design, but it also adds an element of fun and meaning. The brand uses its company name as the base of its logo in a casual and accessible font, but then adds an arrow from the "a" to the "z" in order to signify the enormous amount of inventory it keeps. And while the logo could be considered bland, the use of the fun and energetic orange for the arrow makes it pop. The promise in this logo is that you will find what you need at this exciting website.

Now, let's talk about designing the logo for your own home-based business. Let's start with the basics—the three types of logos that you'll have to choose from.

The Three Types of Logos

There are three main types of logos that you'll be able to choose from when designing yours, but because you run a home-based business, some types stand out above the rest as far as expense and functionality. But before we get into that, here are the three types of logos you'll have to choose from.

- **Word-based logo.** These logos use type treatments to create a logo with a word or company name, and then add something that makes it stand out. The Amazon logo is a perfect example of this type of logo, as is Coca-Cola. (It uses bold red and white colors and a slanted font to differentiate it.)
- **Symbols**. Some logos are merely abstract graphic symbols that, over time, become associated with the brand. Apple's logo falls into this camp, as does Nike's swoosh. On the other hand, some graphic logos represent the real world benefit of the brand, such as a hammer

for a handyman or a swimming pool for a pool cleaning business.
- **Combination logos.** Some logos are a combination of the above two. For instance, McDonalds uses the golden arches combined with its name to convey simple and clean fast food. And Domino's Pizza puts its name on a pizza box, using both a graphic that portrays what it does and its name.

What Logo Type Should Home-Based Businesses Use?

As a home-based business owner, you likely don't have the huge marketing budget that larger corporations do, and that's why you'll need to choose your logo type carefully. You see, while Apple's abstract logo is cool, it took a lot of money to cause consumers to connect it with the brand. The brand's name doesn't appear with the logo and at first glance, the apple graphic has nothing to do with a computer business. Not until you get to know the brand, and then it makes all the sense in the world.

But it took a bucket load of money to cause consumers to make the connection. Something you probably don't have.

That why I suggest you stay away from abstract logos for your home-based business. They're cool and hip yes, but they take a huge budget to pull off, even for a home-based business striving to brand in a smaller environment.

Remember, consumers should be able to tell what you do by the logo you use. And that's why I suggest a combination logo for home-based businesses. With these types of logos, you can choose a graphic that tells your story, and combine it with your name to achieve the best impact.

Think back to our lawn guy. He could design a combination logo using a lawnmower graphic outlined in a "sincere and trustworthy" green, along with his business name in blue. This would convey a reliable lawn service that consumers could count on.

What Makes a Good Logo?

After you've decided on your logo type, you'll need to begin designing it. Don't worry if you don't have graphic artist skills—I'll give you some options later in this chapter. But for now, I'd like you to begin thinking about the graphic that will be the face of your brand. Here are some important points you'll need to keep in mind as you consider it.

- **It must be unique.** In order for your logo to have the most impact, it needs to stand out from the competition and be unique enough that it gets the attention of consumers. Do something out-of-the-box that makes people understand what you do, but at the same time, is so original that they'll remember it.

- **Make it relate to the brand.** While you want your logo to be unique, it shouldn't be so unique that it has nothing to do with the brand—not unless you have a lot of money to spend on marketing. Your logo is an extension of your brand, so be sure it plays the part.
- **Make sure it speaks to your audience.** Remember your ideal customer? Your logo should speak to them in their language. What does that mean? Apple's brand is creative and simple, and the people who typically use its products are creatives. The logo of the simple apple with an unexpected bite taken out of it speaks directly to them. If your brand is emotional, make sure your logo conveys emotions. On the other hand, if it's fun and exciting, design a logo that portrays those characteristics.
- **Keep to your personality color.** Remember, the colors you use should reflect your brand's personality, and that

includes the logo. It's why Apples uses white (simplicity), McDonalds uses red and yellow (exciting and fun), and John Deere uses green. (outdoorsy). And keep in mind that 95 percent of the top brands use only one to two colors.

- **Don't overcomplicate it.** Yes, you want your logo to be eye-catching and interesting, but it needs to be simple at the same time. If you overcomplicate it, you'll lose some of its impact. Ninety-three percent of the top brands are simple enough that consumers can still recognize them in smaller sizes.
- **Make it versatile.** Sometimes you'll be able to display your logo in color, while other times, it will be seen in black and white. Make sure it translates well in both instances, as well as in smaller and larger sizes.
- **Make it adaptable.** While you want a logo that will last throughout the life of your business, you may need to tweak it

now and then to keep up with the times. For example, Coca-Cola has made adjustments to their logo many times over the years, while always keeping the core of the brand the same. Design your logo in a way that will allow slight adjustments with the times.
- **Think long term.** Just because you don't see instant success with your logo, stay the course. It can take some time for a brand to establish itself, and if you get impatient and change the logo, you'll lose out on all the branding momentum you've achieved.

A Word about Typefaces

If you plan to include your company name with a graphic, or use your name as a standalone graphic, you'll need to carefully select your font. It's best to avoid gimmicky fonts and stick with those that other companies have used successfully. For example, brands like JC Penny and Crate & Barrel use Helvetica, which is a simple, all around font. Here is a brief list of some typefaces and the feelings they convey.

- **Serif.** This typeface conveys formality, trust, and maturity.
- **San serif.** If your brand is agreeable, up-to-date and informal, this will work for you.
- **Script.** Is your brand feminine or elaborate and showy? A script font will work for you.
- **Uppercase.** Use this to convey a bold and impactful message.
- **Lowercase.** Using all lowercase letters indicates an informal and relaxed brand.
- **Title case.** If your brand is trustworthy and solid, this is a great choice.

If you need some inspiration or just want to look at all your font choices, check out sites like Font Squirrel, which offers free fonts for commercial use, or HypeForType.

Should You Design Your Logo Yourself?

Before we leave the subject of logos, let's talk about something very important—the design of your logo. There are two schools of thought about whether business owners should design their own logo, and each side has merit.

The naysayers say that only professional designers should design logos because they've been trained in the art and understand how to create a logo that will resonate with consumers and get across the brand's personality. On the other hand, most home-based business owners can't afford to pay a designer thousands of dollars for a logo.

So, what's the answer?

It depends. A lot of home-based business owners are creative and could likely design a logo that would serve their brand well. On the other hand, creativity and graphic design isn't something everyone can do, and if it's not in your wheelhouse, I'd advise you to hire a designer. After all, your logo is the first thing consumers will see, and you have no choice but to get it right.

But you won't have to pay thousands of dollars to get it done, as I'll show you in a minute. First, I'd like to tell you about a few sites you can use if you want to try designing your own logo.

Logo Design Websites

Many small business owners have created impactful logos using logo interfaces available online. If you want to attempt to design your own logo, or if you want to create a prototype for a designer, you can't beat the following websites.

- Logomaker.com. This site allows you create logos free of charge, and if you create a logo you want to use, you'll pay only $39.95 to download the file.
- Logoyes.com. This is another great site that allows you to design your logo for

free, and then charges .99 to download a high resolution file.
- Graphicsprings.com. Another great logo making tool that is free to use. It also offers you the ability to customize your logo in a way that other programs don't. Once you create a logo you like, you'll pay only $19.99 to download it.
- Logoshi. This is an outstanding tool for those of you who want to create a logo with your business name. Simply sketch your rough logo and the software will use your design to create a professionally looking logo. Use it for free and then download your file for $19.
- Logaster. On this site, you can create your logo, and then download a high resolution file for $9.99.

If you don't want to design your own logo, you can either purchase a premade logo at places like brandcrowd.com starting at several hundred dollars, or buy premade logo elements such as fonts, templates, and graphics at creativemarket.com.

And finally, if you want someone else to custom design a logo for your brand from start to finish, you can't do better than 99designs.com. There, you'll create a "contest" where you'll describe what you want. Then at least 10 professional designers will come up with a logo, and you'll be able to select the one you want. Prices start at $299.

Wow, you mean it's possible to avoid spending thousands of dollars on a professionally designed logo and get one for as little as $299? Yep. **Just because you own a home-based business, that doesn't mean you can't run with the big boys as far as branding.**

How to Protect Your Logo

Now that you've put so much work into designing your logo, it's important that you protect it. After all, if you don't, anyone can use it without your consent. If you want some examples of logo rip-offs, check out [LogoThief.com.](http://LogoThief.com) It's full of examples of brazen logo thievery.

Logo thieves can copy or mimic your logo, which is a crime known as trademark infringement. This will cause problems for you because it associates your brand with theirs. In addition, trademark dilution happens when another company uses your brand name or logo in a way that makes it less unique or skews the intent of the brand.

You can avoid potential issues like this by trademarking your brand, adding the "TM" to your logo, and then registering it across the nation. Here are the steps you'll need to take to complete this process.

- Decide what to trademark. You'll need to identify which aspects of your logo are uniquely linked to your brand. Those

symbols or words are what you will trademark.
- Locate the corresponding codes in the Design Search Code Manual, and then use them to determine whether or not they've already been registered by someone else using the Trademark Electronic Search System. If they have, consider hiring an intellectual property attorney to negotiate for you.
- Complete the online application at the United States Patent and Trademark Office. You'll pay a nonrefundable filing fee from $225 to $325 for each category that applies to your logo. You'll be assigned a serial number right away. It's possible to complete the process with a paper application, but it takes a few weeks to obtain the serial number.
- Wait for the response. Your application will either be approved or denied, and if it's denied, you'll be given a full explanation of why. You'll have six

months to respond to the denial, and if you wait longer than that, the application will be considered abandoned by you. If approved, you'll need to file an Affidavit of Use 5 to 6 years afterwards, and then once every 10 years in order to keep your trademark up to date.

There is some debate about whether home-based businesses have to go the trouble of registering their logo and paying the fees every few years. The attorney's at [owe.com](owe.com), who are specialists in intellectual property law, say that if a logo is unregistered, the owners still have the right to be protected from trademark infringements, **but only in the area where the logo is used**. Now, I'm no attorney, but it seems to me that would cover home-based business owners solely operating in a local community even if they don't register their trademark. But before you make a decision about whether or not register your logo, be sure to contact an attorney for clarification.

What do you think? Is your head spinning with ideas and you can't wait to get started branding your home-based business? I think you'll be amazed at how much difference a brand makes when marketing your business. You'll be seen as professional and competent, and many consumers will believe you're bigger than you are because of your professional presentation. And that, my friends, will result in more profit for you.

Next, I'd like to talk about building your Brand Bible. What is it, why is it important, and how do you go about building one? Turn the page for the answers to all of those questions and more!

Chapter Nine: How to Create a Brand Bible—and Why You Shouldn't Skip this Step

Once you've designed and created all the aspects of your brand, it will be tempting to congratulate yourself and then sit back and take a break. But don't. There is one more step to this process that is essential to the success of your brand.

You'll need to create a Brand Bible, also known as a style guide, to direct and monitor the use of your brand for years to come. There are no hard and fast rules for this book, and what yours looks like will depend on your business and goals. For instance, if you plan to stay very small and never venture outside of your immediate geographical area, your book might only be a few pages. But if you operate a home-based internet company and plan to rule the world one day with dozens of employees, your book could end up being a few hundred pages. That's because you'll need a clear guidebook that instructs employees on how to specifically use all the elements of your brand.

What is a Brand Bible?

The book you put together will be used as the guide for exactly how the public views your company. It dictates how the brand will interact with the world via its social media accounts, marketing efforts, designs, and personal communications. And it's extremely useful if you need to hire a designer to update your logo or create an advertising campaign. In other words, it's the playbook for your brand's interactions with the world at large.

Let's take a look at some of the essential elements for your Brand Bible.

State Your Goals

The first you should do in your Brand Bible is to clearly state the company's goals and philosophy. This is important information to know, and these two things will guide everything you do as a brand in the years to come.

Outline Your Logo Usage

Next, you'll need to set some clear guidelines about how your logo should be used. For example, you'll need to define where it can be used, whether or not it can be used in black and white, where it should be placed on a page, what sizes are acceptable, how much white space should be around it, and whether or not there are any acceptable alterations.

Don't forget to include important information in this section such as what your preferred marketing tactics are, and those you want to avoid. Also include the proper spelling of your company name and tagline.

Decide on Typography and Font Usage

Every communication your business puts out should look exactly the same. That's true whether you're sending out an email, a letter, running an ad or using a magnetic sign on your car. Consistency in a brand is important, and that includes the use of fonts and typography.

In this section, you'll want to define how to use typography, which typefaces are to be used and in what manner, and how to approach sizes, add-on styling, and the use of color in your typography.

Finally, you'll want to select your typefaces—most brands have a primary and a complementary one—and then set guidelines for them. When should each be used? Perhaps you will specify one for print advertising and one for your digital communications, and it's wise to list back up typefaces just in case.

Specify Your Colors

You've already selected your colors, but now it's time to get more specific. You'll need to define your color palette for not only your logo, but for all of your advertising and communications. This section should specify each color associated with your brand, and then define exactly how that color is to be used. For example, you'll need to identify the colors used in your logo, image backgrounds, and text. (Be sure to select primary, secondary, and alternative colors for your palette.) These colors can include a combination of tints and fully saturated versions.

Finally, be sure to mark each color by name and color value for each type of project you can foresee. Use the CMYK color model for print projects and the RGB color model for digital applications. And if you're using Pantone colors, be sure to note their assigned values.

Create Image Guidelines

In this section, you'll need to set guidelines as to how images are to be used in your brand's communications. Will you use photography in your advertising efforts, or illustrations, clip art, or graphics? How will you source the images, and how will they be edited and used in the final product? Will you use color images or black and white?

This section should be used to define exactly what role images will play in your brand communications and advertising efforts.

Decide on Your Brand's Tone

Remember I told you that your brand personality would carry over into everything you do? In this section, you'll identify and create guidelines for exactly how the brand will "communicate." For instance, if you issue a press release, what tone should it be written in? What about your blog posts? You'll need identify the acceptable (and unacceptable) language for all of your communications because your brand should always "sound" the same to consumers.

Here are some of the considerations you'll need to think about:

- Will your communications be simple and succinct or wordy and elaborate?

- Should your tone be informal and casual or formal?
- Will you use descriptive words and phrases or pared down and easy-to-understand sentences?

When you know who your ideal customer is (and you do, right?) then it will be easy to create this section of your Brand Bible because you should aim to speak directly to them.

In addition to all of the above specifications, your Brand Bible should include guidelines for every single aspect of your business brand. For example, be sure to include information for the following areas:

- The history of your brand.
- Your vision for the brand's future.
- The brand USP
- The brand personality
- Logo specs and instructions for how to use it
- Typography specifications
- Color palette
- Image guidelines

- Business card design
- Letterhead design
- Design samples and grids for digital advertisements
- Design samples and grids for print advertisements
- Guidelines for brochures
- Guidelines and specifications for outdoor advertising and signage
- Tone of voice and writing style guidelines
- Guidelines for how the brand will interact with consumers on social media

I know—this is a lot, and it can be overwhelming to think about putting together such a book, but as a brand owner, you will quickly see the wisdom in doing it.

Imagine for a moment that you're participating in a community event and the organizer wants to include your brand in a special pull out section of the newspaper. How much easier would it be if you could refer her to your Brand Bible for the specifications on how your logo is to be used?

If you need some more motivation and inspiration to create your Brand Bible, check out the online bibles of brands such as Skype, easy.com, and Adobe. For a list of 83 more

Brand Bibles of popular brands, see this article at logodesignlove.com. (For those of you reading this in paperback, the links are https://download.skype.com/share/blogskin/press/skype_brandbook.pdf , http://www.easy.com/PDFs/easyGroup_Brand_Manual.pdf, http://brandcenterdl.adobe.com/Corpmktg/Brandmktg/Campaign_Assets/guidelines/corporate/corporate_brand_guidelines.pdf , and http://www.logodesignlove.com/brand-identity-style-guides

Remember, the goal of your Brand Bible is to create a unified front for your brand's personality. It should outline the way you, and everyone else associated with your company, presents the brand to the world. A well-constructed Brand Bible will go a long way in ensuring that your brand is consistent in the eyes of the public.

Well, you now have a brand that you can use to forge those all-important relationships with consumers and begin growing your home-based business. But how do you use your brand to grow your business? After all, you operate in a smaller environment than big business, so the same brand marketing techniques won't work the same, right?

Let's move on to our final chapter where I'll tell you exactly how to use your new brand to grow your business—on a local level.

Chapter Ten: How to Grow Your Home-Based Business Using Your New Brand

So, how does it feel? You've designed and created a brand for your home-based business that will not only set you apart from your competitors, but it will allow you to interact with local consumers in a way that will cause them to become loyal to your brand. Congratulations—you are well on your way to becoming the local go-to business in your community.

But now that you have your brand, what are some of the real world steps you can take to use it to help grow your business?

Why, I just so happen to have a few pointers for you. Here are some of the best ways you can use your new brand to grow your business.

Use Your Brand to Add Credibility

Now that your business is branded, it has advantages over your competitors who haven't yet taken this important step. For instance, your advertisements will be cohesive and structured in a way that promotes and strengthens your brand in the community. But don't stop there.

Sometimes your position as a home-based business can help in the local community because people like to buy from their neighbors, but even those people expect professionalism and a sense of competency in the businesses they buy from. In other words, your brand will work to make your business more credible in the eyes of consumers, but in order to most take advantage of that momentum, you should carry it through to other aspects of your business. Here are some ways to do that.

- **Your website.** If it's been a few years since you updated your website, now is the time to do it. Ensure that it reflects your current branding and is user-friendly for your customers. A poorly maintained website, or one that stays stagnant and outdated, screams of a small business.

Customers will look to your website as validation that you are a business worth patronizing.

- **Your communications**. One of the biggest hurdles small business owners face is looking small because of communication limitations. For example, taking a phone call while your child is crying in the other room or using homemade business cards will instantly make you lose credibility in some consumer's eyes. Instead, invest in the things that will make your business appear more polished and professional. Redo your business cards with your branding, lose the free email and use one connected to your website address, use a branded email signature line, and hire a virtual receptionist to answer calls when you can't, or want them routed to you after being answered. VoIP phone services like CallRuby.com and MoneyPenny.com are geared toward small business owners and won't break the bank.

Partner With Another Brand

Another way to grow your brand is to step outside of your comfort zone and partner with a similar (but non-competitive) company. This will expose you to more potential customers and get your brand in front of more people.

For example, our landscape owner could partner with a pool cleaning business and offer customers a discount if they use both services. When partnering with another brand, you should make sure the brand has a great reputation because by working together, your business will take on its reputation.

Use Referrals

Can you imagine what would happen if all of your customers referred their friends, neighbors, and family to your business? Your sales would go through the roof and so would your brand visibility. A smart way to accomplish this is to offer customers something in return for a referral.

I have a friend who owns a home-based interior design business and she used this model to grow her business. She offered her customers and Realtors a $25 reward for every new customer they sent her. The result? Her business tripled, and she soon became known as the designer who did entire streets in a neighborhood.

Design a system that rewards customers and others for sending you business and you will create a community of brand ambassadors to help spread word of your business.

Become the Expert

If you can become known as the local expert in your industry, your brand's visibility will skyrocket. How can a home-based business owner do this? You can offer to write a column for your local newspaper, and create a blog on your own website, and then point local customers to it for information. In addition, you can offer free classes to teach consumers something about your industry and get yourself branded as an expert.

You can also write guest posts on blogs related to your industry in order to expand your brand. Buffer used this strategy and wrote 150 guest posts for other blogs and grew their user base from zero to over 100,000 in only nine months.

Host Local Webinars

Think webinars are just for those business with a national customer base? Think again. Local home-based business owners can seriously expand the reach of their brand by hosting local webinars in their area. Instead of having to make your sales pitches one-by-one, you could host a webinar and do it all at once across the entire city. This works especially well in large cities because it allows a convenient way for you to reach people who may not want to make the drive to your business. And if you offer a way for attendees to sign up or order the product electronically after the webinar, it would be even better.

Another way to expand your brand's reach by using webinars is to invite existing customers to one every time you add a new product or service and want to fill them in on the details. It will keep your brand's name at the forefront of their minds whenever they are in need of your products or services.

Get Publicity

Another great way to get your brand name in front of locals to get the media talking about you. In order to do this successfully, you'll need to think outside the box. For example, before Uber was so well-known, it gave free rides to well-connected attendees at tech events. And when those people shared their experiences via social media, Uber's brand took off. The possibilities are endless for home-based business owners to take advantage of this technique. For example, our lawn guy could commit to mowing the local courthouse for free every week for a year. That's something the local journalists would love to write about.

Community Events

Local brands that spend their time with the community participating in local events quickly build their brand. You can do this by participating in fundraisers, charity events, or by putting on your own workshops or classes. However you do it, mingling with the locals is a great strategy for a home-based business brand because it helps build trust with them.

Use Social Media—Locally

Finally, the absolute best way to get visibility for your brand is to use social media. In today's world, social media is the king as far as reaching consumers and building awareness for your brand. But the rules continue to change every day for social media engagement, and if you want to use the platforms to grow your brand, you'll have to learn them quickly.

One of the biggest benefits to expanding your brand via social media is that it doesn't cost a lot of money. That's why so many brands these days spend so much of their marketing efforts on it.

And here's the best part: you can use social media in your local area just as well as the big companies that reach across the globe. In fact, the very core of what social media is is an extension of what makes local communities so great. It's a place where you can gather with your customers and prospective customers and mingle. You'll have a public conversation with them, which allows you to get to know each other.

But the one thing social media is **not** is a sales pitch. It's not a place to tell consumers how great your product or service is, and it's definitely not a place to ask them to buy it. After all, when you're mingling at a local event, what is your reaction when someone uses the conversation to try and sell you something? Social media users have the same reaction.

But as a home-based business owner, if done right, you can leverage the power of social media and use it just as effectively as larger companies. In fact, you can use many of their proven concepts right in your own background to grow your brand. But you'll need a concrete strategy to make the best use out of this marketing medium.

Remember when we talked about your brand story earlier in the book? Social media is the place where you'll share that story and express your brand personality. Your brand is ultimately created by customer experience, and social media is the place where you will try to exert some control over that conversation. Your brand identity with your logo, colors and texts are a vital and necessary part of your brand, but brands that experience true success also learn how to interact with consumers using real-time engagement and conversations that inspire them, make them think, and drive them to action. But it all must be done in a human way using your brand personality.

First, Build a Following

Your first step in using social media to build your brand is to build a following of loyal, interested people. The key here is interested—if your followers aren't truly interested in what you have to say, you're just wasting your time. All those businesses that buy fake followers? Yes, they have "social proof," but their marketing efforts are simply wasted.

It's much better to build an organic following of people in your local area who care about what you have to say. But despite what some marketing "experts" say, building a true audience of followers takes time. The thing to remember is that you can't expect to post one great piece of content and have hundreds of people follow you. Remember, earning the trust of consumers is the goal, and no one does that overnight.

The best place to start building your following is by asking your customers which social media sites they use. You can ask them in person when they're at the checkout counter, in an email, or on the phone. Once you determine which site most of your customers are on, set up a business account on it and begin spreading the news.

After that, you'll need to continually post engaging content in order to get people to follow you. Below, I've outlined each of the major social media sites, and talk about how local businesses can make the best use of them.

Facebook

Did you know that more than 75 percent of the adult population in the U.S. uses the social media giant on a regular basis? In all, there are 1.5 billion users on Facebook, and 40 percent of users use Facebook as a check in service for the local businesses they frequent. And if your customer base consists of senior citizens or women, Facebook should definitely be a priority in your marketing plans as 50 percent of its users are senior citizens and 75 percent of all U.S. women have an account with the service. And of its users, 65 percent of them check in to their Facebook page every single day.

Wow—that's a lot of people who use this platform, and chances are, a good many of them are in your local area. As a home-based business owner, you would do well to put your time and marketing efforts into this site. And because the platform is so well geared toward businesses that want to advertise to local users, it launched its new [Local Awareness Ads](#) to help local business target local customers. The ads show up to people who are located near your business.

How else can you use the platform to build your brand? Here are a few ways local businesses have succeeded in using the site.

It's all About Content

In order to build your brand and elicit loyalty from local customers, you'll need to express your personality on your Facebook page via great content and photos. In fact, studies have shown that content with photos are liked and shared more often. But you can't just repost interesting stories and expect to gain a following. Instead, you'll need to create original content on your blog and then post it to your Facebook page. And you can use free sites like Canva.com to create perfectly sized photos for your posts.

You can also engage your fans by creating contests on your Facebook, such as "caption the photo" contests. With them, you'll post an interesting photo and then ask your followers to come up with a caption for it. You can include a giveaway for the best caption or simply allow your followers to have fun on your site.

Videos are another great way to add content to your Facebook page, and these days it only takes a smartphone to make one. For example, [Point Reyes Farmstead Cheese](#) posted a video titled "About a Sandwich," that highlighted their product in an engaging and mouthwatering manner.

Newsjacking is another trend that has really taken off in the past few years. Brands that stay on top of breaking stories can highjack those stories to draw attention to their brand. But unless done properly, this can backfire. For instance, an example of this done well happened when Kate Middleton gave birth to her son. Oreo created this photo and posted it on their social media channels.

This is an excellent example of a brand newsjacking a story with class. On the other hand, some attempts at the technique haven't turned out so well.

 **@KennethCole**
Kenneth Cole

Millions are in uproar in #Cairo. Rumor is they heard our new spring collection is now available online at http://bit.ly/KCairo -KC

3 hours ago via Twitter for BlackBerry® ☆ Favorite ⋈ Retweet ↰ Reply

The above photo is an example of what NOT to do when newsjacking a story. The rules of thumb are easy, don't jack a story that involves the suffering of others or your brand will come across as coldhearted and self-serving.

Finally, you can engage your followers by asking them for feedback about specific issues. For example, if you're thinking about carrying a new product and want to know the thoughts of your customers, create a post (with a photo of the new product) and ask for feedback. This will make them feel a part of your brand and cause them to interact with it.

Twitter

If your ideal customer is between the ages of 18 and 29 years old, you should be on Twitter as that age group makes up the vast majority of it 49 million U.S. users. (Keep in mind that 55 percent of Twitter users also use Instagram, so if you're going to use Twitter, you should think about using that site as well.)

In fact, adults only make up about 20 percent of the social media platform, but one-half of all Millennials use the site regularly. The site allows local businesses to interact with customers, quickly answer questions and receive feedback, and easily promote their latest product releases and news. But since 75 percent of its users access it via a mobile device, you'll need to make sure your postings all translate to those types of devices.

Just like with most social media sites, if you only promote your product or talk about yourself, you'll have a difficult time finding followers or connecting with them.

Not every local business will do well with Twitter, but it can be a great outlet for some businesses. For instance, a food truck with a dedicated following can do well on the site by tweeting out their location every time they move.

But a plumbing service will likely see no benefit from tweeting about the latest sink styles.

If you decide to use the site, here are some ways to make it the most beneficial for your brand.

- **Follow the right people.** In order to find people to follow, you should use the [advanced search](#) section on Twitter. Simply type in a keyword that is related to your business or industry and fill in the "near this place," field. You'll then be shown a list of people you should consider following.
- **Use Apps.** Sites like [Hootsuite](#) allow you manage your Twitter account by sorting your followers into categories, scheduling tweets in advance, or setting up alerts when a certain keyword is tweeted.
- **Get Mobile.** Download the Twitter mobile app for either your [Android phone](#) or [Apple iOS](#).
- **Observe.** Because Twitter conversations are unique and one wrong move can

seriously hurt your brand, you should begin by simply observing the way others interact on the site. Then once you get the hang of it, you can begin to engage.
- **Engage.** Most experts agree that when you interact as a brand on Twitter, you should tweet original content a third of the time, retweet others a third of the time, and engage in subtle self-promotion a third of the time.

How to Build Engagement on Twitter

After you've set up your Twitter account and learned how to use it, you'll need to begin interacting with your followers. Here are some ways to do that.

- You should start by letting everyone know about your new account. Use your @handle in your email communications, post it in your store, and tell customers as you interact with them.

- Next, you should make it exciting for people to follow you. For instance, you can post limited deals that are only good for a few hours or a day and people will likely retweet them. It's a great way to build brand engagement with your current customers and attract new followers and potential customers.
- Make your business human by posting intriguing photos of what you do. For example, if you run a home-based daycare center, post a photo of the new playground set you just purchased. Or if you run a home-based bakery, post a photo of cookies fresh out of the oven.
- If you can commit to being accessible to your Twitter followers, you can use it as a form of customer service communication. Encourage your followers to contact you directly on Twitter with any questions or concerns. If you can't commit to answering the comments almost instantly,

don't offer this as it may do more harm than good.
- Finally, you can use Twitter as a source of feedback the same way you can do it with Facebook. Ask questions about your business or something going on in the local community and interact with followers as they respond.

Pinterest

If your business caters to women or moms, you need to set up a business Pinterest account and begin promoting your business there. But this site isn't like other social media sites where you simply post or Tweet interesting blogs or messages to the masses. When you own a Pinterest account, you'll develop boards, and only those people who are specifically looking for pins in that category will see them. You can promote your best pins to targeted users using the site's Promoted Pins, and drive people to your website.

Pinterest can be a great help to local business owners trying to develop a following and I'll show you some examples of local businesses that have successfully used it.

Currently there are more than 50 million US users on Pinterest and 90 percent of those users are women and moms, and many of them are affluent. Interestingly enough, 1 in 7 Pinterest users use Facebook to connect to their Pinterest accounts. According to the site, there are over 750 million boards and 30 billion pins on the site. That means you'll have to do some homework to find the best places to pin yours.

The most often shared pins have to do with fashion, arts and crafts, travel, photography, holiday images and recipes, and home décor, but people have had success with a variety of boards.

If Pinterest is a social media site you want to explore, take the following steps to get some awareness for your brand.

- **Study it**. The site is so large and contains so many pins that at first glance it would be impossible to find your way around. But Pinterest has made it easy search for categories on the site. Click to the right of the search box and you'll open a drop down menu that lists the categories. Select the ones that relate to your business and figure out where you'll fit in on the site. You can use the site's [Guided Search](#) to help you narrow down categories, which shows you the most commonly searched words and phrases for your keywords. Once you begin looking at the listed boards, you'll find boards from people who fit into your ideal customer profile.
- **Sign up**. Because you'll be building your brand on the site, you'll need to sign up for a [business account](#). This will give you access to things personal accounts don't have, such as analytics. You'll be asked to fill in your name, a short 160 word profile

description, upload a photo and add your website address. If you want your first follower, follow me at https://www.pinterest.com/samkerns0836/ and I'll follow you back!

- **Build your boards.** Now that you have a good idea what the site is about and what your ideal customers are looking for, it's time to begin building your boards. You should name your boards with the keywords your ideal customers look for, and create a few of them in order to draw the most number of followers. For example, our landscape guy could create boards for lawn care tips, fall landscape ideas, and tree trimming ideas. Be sure to use the relevant keywords in your profile, board titles, and descriptions.
- **Begin sharing.** Now it's time to get creative and start sharing the things your ideal customers are looking for. Make your boards as interesting as you can so you'll attract the attention of those people

who could turn into customers. Remember, the more repins you get, the people will be exposed to your boards. Because you're a locally based business, you should create some boards that are related to your community. For instance, you could create boards that share local events, or other boards that are only relevant to your area. For example, if our landscape guy lived in South Texas, he could create boards about native plants in the area.

- **Develop content.** In addition to repining content from others, develop your own educational content that will help your followers learn more about your business. For instance, the landscape guy could create an infographic about how to plant fruit trees in the fall. You could also write a blog post and pin it, or create a simple explainer video to show people how to do something. Keep in mind vertical pins do best on the site that are sized at 600 x 1200 pixels. And don't forget to write a caption using your keywords to cause people to repin it more.

- **Use rich pins.** It's possible to embed information from your website into pins, which will help convert pinners to customers. Rich pins take some tech know-how, so you if you aren't tech savvy, you may need the help of a developer.
- **Be personable.** Just like any other social media channel, the key to success is allowing consumers to engage with your brand. If someone asks you a question, answer right away, and include your own comments on other people's pins and boards. Remember, your brand personality should shine in every engagement.
- **Analyze your efforts.** As you continue to build your platform on Pinterest, you'll want to pay attention to the analytics to determine how you're doing. If you set up

a business profile, you'll have this important data at your fingertips.

Meetup.com

Finally, Meetup is an excellent tool for local business owners, but not one that you hear about too often. The site has about 20 million users spread across the United States, and it allows individuals and business owners to organize events and networking opportunities in their local area.

The possibilities with this site are endless for local business owners. You could create a monthly meetup for local business owners so you could network together, form partnerships, or plan community events. Or you could devise meetup for customers to inform them about new products or services, celebrate a local event, or host classes or workshops.

The site is searchable by location and event type, but in order to ensure you success as the host of a meetup, you'll need to heavily promote it directly to your customers and on all your social media sites. About ten thousand local groups meet using the site every day, and over 500,000 meetups happen each month. If you want to host a meetup for your local business, it will only cost $12.

Those are the most important social media sites for local, home-based business owners, but depending on your type of business, there are plenty more to choose from. My millennial-aged son summed up social media perfectly when he realized I was writing this chapter.

- Put your brand on every social media site you can because it will give you more opportunities to attract fans.
- Connect all your social media accounts and brand them consistently.
- You don't have to post on all the sites every day, but do it often.
- Reach out to people who can help your business in some way, but only ask after

communicating with them in a friendly way.
- Be a person, not a business in your communications.

And there you have it—straight from the horse's mouth.

So, how do you feel? Do you think you have a grip on how to best brand your home-based business? If you've read the book and applied all the tips and advice I've given you, you should be well on your way to boosting your business visibility and credibility in your local community.

As always, I love to hear from readers and answer emails and website comments personally. If you have any, you can either find me at RainMakerPress.com (where you can also sign up for information about new releases, special deals and more) or via email at SamKernsBooks@gmail.com.

And **please**, if you've enjoyed the book, [please leave a review on Amazon](). Reviews help authors like me stand out on Amazon, and also help other people decide whether or not to buy a book.

And don't forget, on the next few pages I've provided a brief summary of the other four books in this series, including [*How to Publish a Book on Amazon: Real Advice from Someone Who's Doing it Well,*]() which is available for pre-order now.

Until next time, get out there and pursue your dreams!

Sam

Other Books in the Work from

Home Series by Sam Kerns

I hope you enjoyed this book and use it to design and create a successful brand for your home-based business. As promised, here's a list of the first four books in the Work from Home Series, as well as some information about my newest book, *How to Publish a Book on Amazon: Real Advice from Someone Who's Doing it Well*.

I hope you find something you like!

How to Work From Home and Make Money: 10 Proven Home-Based Businesses You Can Start Today (Work from Home Series: Book 1)

Life is Too Short to Work for Someone Else!

Are you tired of struggling just to get by with a paycheck that doesn't quite stretch far enough? Or are you one of the millions of people who are out of work in an economy gone bad? Maybe you long to be your own boss so you can set your own schedule and choose the path your life will take.

Whatever it is that brought you to this page, you're obviously looking for answers. **The good news is you've come to the right place.**

I've spent the past 20 years working for myself, and I would never dream of punching another clock or trudging to someone else's office every day to collect a meager paycheck. That's because I've discovered the secret: when you work for yourself, you're happier, more productive, and you have unlimited earning potential.

After all, **why would you want to work so hard to fund someone else's dreams?**

Working for myself has allowed me to live a lifestyle that many people can only dream about. I have the flexibility to create the life I want, take days off when I need to, and I decide how much money I make by choosing the hours I work.

But don't be fooled. Working from home at a home-based business isn't easy. It takes hard work and dedication to build a successful business that will make money.

In my book, I'm pleased to offer you **10 proven, realistic ways to work from home and earn a great income.** And I won't just offer you a brief explanation of each method like some other books do.

In each chapter, I provide you with the information and facts you need to determine if that business is right for you. But I don't stop there. I'll also give you important links and resources, so if you decide you want to pursue one of the home-based business ideas listed in this book, **you'll have everything you need to begin.**

So, the choice is yours. Will you wake up tomorrow morning and spend your day funding someone else's dream, or will you finally take the steps needed to claim your own success?

Why not start right now by buying How to Work From Home and Make Money? It's one of the most important things you'll do to begin the process of achieving your own dreams.

Buy the Book on Amazon!

How to Build a Writing Empire in 30 Days or Less (Work from Home Series: Book 2)

How to Build a
WRITING
EMPIRE in
30 Days or Less

Sam Kerns

Do You Want to Make a Real Living as a Writer? You'll Have to Throw Out Everything You Know

Let me guess—you're a talented writer who is willing to do whatever it takes to make a full-time living by writing. You've read countless articles and books on the subject, followed the suggestions in them, but you just can't seem to make the income leap.

Or you may be a new writer who is convinced that you're missing something because your own experience isn't matching up to what you've read is possible.

Or perhaps you've been moonlighting as a freelance writer for years, and you're convinced that it's simply not possible to quit your "real" job and do what you love full time.

Let me tell you a secret. You've been lied to. Yes, you heard me correctly. **Lied. To.**

The truth is, only about 10 percent of writers earn enough working full time to support themselves. *Ten percent.* That's not something all those other how-to writing books spend a lot of time on, is it?

Luckily, there's a real solution.

I know this because I've been doing it myself for years. But in order to be successful in this business, you'll have to turn the current freelance writing working model on its head. In fact, you pretty much **have to throw everything you thought you knew out the window.**

What I'm talking about is a new system. One that doesn't limit a freelance writer's ability to make a great income because of time constraints. I'm talking about earning a living anyone would be proud of.

In this book, I'll show you how to create your own Writing Empire in 30 days or less. You'll learn:

- Why most freelancers can't make a decent living—and what to do about it
- How to structure your writing business in a way that works best for your lifestyle
- How to brand your business to attract the type of clients you want
- Where to find clients and how to land the jobs
- How to structure your time in order to earn the highest possible income in the shortest amount of time
- How to hire a team of qualified, motivated writers who will help you build your Empire

And that's not all. I'll give you a **step-by-step plan** that will lead you to success. This plan looks **in detail** at your first:

- Day
- Week
- Month
- And beyond

Like I said, I structured my own business this way, so let my experience help you achieve your dreams.

Are you ready to get serious about your writing career and make some serious money? Start right now by downloading the book and learn how to make a real living with writing!

Buy the Book on Amazon!

How to Start a Home-Based Food Business: Turn Your Foodie Love into Serious Cash with a Food Business Startup (Work from Home Series Book 3)

Finally, a Comprehensive Guide to Starting a Food Business!

Do your insides jump for joy when you see a perfectly frosted cupcake or cookie? Or do you love the look of violet lavender syrup or a mouthwatering strawberry and lime jam? Or are you more of a savory person and melt when you see a jar of homemade salsa or seasoned nuts with just the right amount of spices?

If food excites you as much as it does me, you just might be a foodie. And in today's food-centered world, there is serious money to be made with your passion.

Food consumption has really changed in the past decade, and now more than ever, people want to know what's in their food, where it came from and who made it. That's bad news for businesses that mass produce food, but great news for those in the cottage food industry.

You see, in the past individuals who wanted to sell food were required to involve the state health inspectors and lease commercial kitchens in order to sell to the public. Obviously, that prevented a lot of people from pursuing their food dreams. But now many states have passed **cottage food laws** that are designed to give home chefs and bakers the right to produce products from their homes and sell them to the public.

If you've read my other books, you know I'm a serial entrepreneur. I've opened and closed many businesses in my lifetime, and there's nothing I love more than taking an idea and turning it into a smoothly run, profitable business. And this book was born of that desire.

Let me explain.

I bake. There—it's out in the open. I'm a guy and I bake.

Can we please move on?

Specifically, I bake specialty brownies that are so good I've had local stores approach me and ask me to sell them wholesale, and I get phone calls from friends begging me to bake a batch. Yeah, my brownies are that good.

So when I heard about the changes in the law allowing people to start home-based food businesses, my entrepreneurial mind starting spinning. I have a great product, so in my mind, there was no reason why I couldn't create a profitable business. I should just open one, right?

Fortunately, that's not the way I roll. I have never simply opened a business and learned as I go—instead I conduct so much research that I know absolutely everything there is to know before I begin. In other words, I leave no room for error. I want the information up front so I can make the best decisions and build a successful business.

Otherwise, what's the point?

So, when the idea of opening a cottage food business occurred to me, I began researching and I didn't stop for months. That's where this book comes in. There is a lot to know about this type of business, and one thing I learned is that there is simply nowhere that you can get all of the information in one place.

Until this book.

Don't believe me? Take a look at all the other books on the subject and just see if the author provides a state-by-state index of all the cottage food laws. Let me save you some time. They don't.

And recipes that fit into the guidelines of the laws? Nope, you won't find them in other books. How about serious insight into how to best brand, package and market your home-based food business? You'll only find that in this book.

So, let my obsessive research into business ideas, along with my entrepreneurial skills, help you in your own business. I've done the hard work for you, so **all you have do is follow the plan I've outlined in this book and you'll be on your way to building your very own food business**. And all the newbie questions you have but are too embarrassed to ask? I had them, too and I've included the answers to them in this book.

If you're ready to pursue your foodie dreams, download the book and learn everything you need to know!

Buy the Book on Amazon!

And my latest book:

How to Publish a Book on Amazon: Real Advice from

Someone Who's Doing it Well (Work from Home Series: Book 5)

How to Publish a Book on Amazon: Real Advice from Someone Who's Doing it Well

Sam Kerns

Are you tired of "how to publish books" that are full of fluff and no real information? I was, too.

Before I began my publishing career with Kindle books, I read just about everything out there, looking for real answers to questions I had about the industry. But much to my disappointment, most of the books were filled with fluff or stories of people who "hit it big" without really telling me how or why.

I determined to jump in and learn for myself—and that's exactly what I did. I started with my first book, How to Work from Home and Make Money, and then quickly published three more. I was looking for the topic of my fifth book when it hit me—**why not share what I've learned with the people who still haven't made the leap and published their own book?**

It all began when I received an email from a book promotion site. One of the features was a how to book about publishing Kindle books, so out of curiosity, I followed the link and read the reviews. And sure enough, the page was full of people complaining that the book didn't contain any valuable information.

So here's what I decided to do. Write a book that answers all of the real questions without painting an unrealistic view of the possibilities. I answer things like:

- How to pick book topics that will sell. (Why it's important, and what I've done right—and wrong.)
- How to write a book in 30 days or less. (And take weekends off)
- How to conduct research for your book.
- How to make your own covers for free.

- The pros and cons of pre-releasing your book.
- When you should enroll your book in Kindle Unlimited (And when you shouldn't.)
- How to format your book yourself. (Including the clickable table of contents) And how to get it done for cheap if you don't want to.
- Why you need a paperback version. (And how to create one)
- Why you may need an audio book (And how to get one for free)
- How to get your book translated into other languages for free (And why you should)
- Why ranking matters (And what to do if your book isn't ranking well.)
- How to market your book. (Including links and contact information for the people I use)
- What to do after you publish your first book.
- How much you can REALLY expect to make with Kindle publishing

I talk about the mistakes I've made so you don't make them, too. And I provide you with **step-by-step instructions and relevant links for all of the above areas**—and more. In other words, this book is the ONLY book you'll need to start a career publishing Kindle books.

If you've been dreaming of publishing a book, but don't know where to start—or if you've already published but can't find success—this may be the book you've been waiting for.

Why not take the first step toward your publishing career and download it right now? I promise you won't find any fluff or useless information in it. Just an actionable guide that answers the questions no one else will.

Buy the book on Amazon!

Thank you for downloading

How to Brand Your Home-Based Business: Why Business Branding is Crucial for Even the Smallest Startups
(The Work from Home Series: Book 4)

Sign up at my website RainMakerPress.com for special offers, promotions, and information about new releases in this series.

www.ingramcontent.com/pod-product-compliance
Lightning Source LLC
Chambersburg PA
CBHW070229190526
45169CB00001B/134